C000221650

LABOUR, THE AN
& THE DESTR(

Lee Garratt was born in 1972, in Manchester, England. He graduated in 1995 from the University of Greenwich with a Humanities degree and obtained his English secondary PGCE in 2004 from St Martin's College. He has been a barman, a TEFL teacher, a holiday tour guide and Metropolitan Police constable. He is the eldest child of a transport worker and secretary and currently works as an English secondary school teacher in the East Midlands. He is the author of one political work (*Labour, the anti-Semitism Crisis & the Destroying of an MP*) and has had a variety of books published including the fantasy novella *Remains* and two short story collections: *New Worlds* and *Other Times, Distant Lands.*

'Corbyn – he did not present a threat only to Israel and Israel's supporters. He posed a threat to the whole British elite. Across the board from *The Guardian* to the *Daily Mail*, they all joined in the new anti-Semitism campaign. Now, that's unprecedented - the entire British elite during this whole completely contrived, fabricated, absurd and obscene assault on this alleged Labour anti-Semitism, of which there is exactly zero evidence.'

Norman Finkelstein

'I've never recognised [anti-Semitism]. I believe it was mood music that was created by people who were trying to undermine Jeremy Corbyn...In 47 years of membership of the Labour Party, I've never been at a meeting where there was any anti-Semitic language or any attacks on the Jewish nation. They would have had short shrift.'

Len McCluskey

'It is becoming more and more clear that Israel is losing control over liberal public opinion and is compelled to rely for support on the most reactionary elements and the fundamentalist Evangelical movement, which combines fervent support for the most extreme Israeli actions ...Authentic antisemites, I presume, are delighted to see Jews self-ridiculed in this fashion, while others should be shuddering at the spectacle. That's not of course to deny that one can ferret out strains of antisemitism in the Labour Party [but] levels [in] England, so general studies have indicated, [are] quite low by historical standards and vastly below hatred of Muslims and other prevalent forms of racism.'

Noam Chomsky

'If you want to understand how accusations of anti-Semitism were used to undermine the most radical political movement in the history of the post-war labour movement, you have to read *Labour, the anti-Semitism Crisis & the Destroying of an MP*. Chris Williamson's removal from parliamentary politics is a lesson in corruption, weakness and courage that we all need to learn from.'

Jackie Walker

'[Keir Starmer] made a commitment regarding what I [see] not as [a] witch-hunt [but] really a heresy hunt. They don't burn us, they excommunicate us.'

Moshé Machover

'No wonder Labour anti-Semitism got the 'Panorama' treatment – Tory racism is way too much to fit into an hour…Conservative members love politicians who protect the kind of British life a person can relate to, such as wearing a monocle and having 19 kids you never see until they've left Eton.'

Mark Steel

Lee Garratt

LABOUR,
THE ANTI-SEMITISM
CRISIS
&
THE DESTROYING
OF AN MP

THINKWELL BOOKS

Edited by Jeff Weston.

Front cover design by Ammar Kazmi.

Interior formatting by Rachel Bostwick.

Published by Thinkwell Books, U.K.

First printing edition 2021.

Dedicated to comrades in Britain and around the world

We have a world to win

"There are no facts, only interpretations"

- Friedrich Nietzsche

Notebooks, Summer 1886 - Autumn 1887

Table of Contents

Glossary 1

Foreword 3

Preface 5

Introduction 11

1 - The Manufactured anti-Semitism 'Crisis' 13

2 - The Strange Tale of Luciana Berger 33

3 - Chris Williamson - The Making of a Socialist 39

4 - High Court - Justice Served? 69

5 - Starmer, Panorama and the Leaked Report 81

6 - The EHRC Report 91

7 - With Friends Like These 103

Conclusion with Finkelstein 117

Afterword 125

Appendices 133

Endnotes 207

GLOSSARY

BoD - Board of Deputies of British Jews

CAA – Campaign Against Antisemitism

CLP – Constituency Labour Party

CLPD – Campaign for Labour Party Democracy

EHRC – Equality and Human Rights Commission

GLU – Governance and Legal Unit (of the Labour Party)

IHRA – International Holocaust Remembrance Alliance

JLM - Jewish Labour Movement

JVL - Jewish Voice for Labour

LFI - Labour Friends of Israel

NEC – The Labour Party's National Executive Committee

PLP - Parliamentary Labour Party

SCG – Socialist Campaign Group of Labour MPs

FOREWORD - by Tommy Sheridan

This book is essential reading for anyone interested in the anatomy of power in society and the ability of vested interests within the corrupted and corrosive mainstream media to manipulate, mislead and maliciously malign in the cause of self-preservation (thus defending the grotesque income and power inequality which serves the elites so well).

Examination of the political contributions of the likes of Jeremy Corbyn, Ken Livingstone and Chris Williamson throughout their lengthy careers in pursuit of social justice and socialism domestically and internationally leaves you in no doubt that these men are champions of equality and anti-racist to the core. Their political DNA compels them to oppose all forms of discrimination with courage and gusto. These are individuals who have not just talked about taking on racism, intolerance, anti-Semitism and hate throughout their lives - they have taken to the streets to physically stand against the fascists and hate-mongers in their many ugly forms.

Yet the creation of a narrative during the last decade that casts these men as anti-Semites underlines the preposterous and perverse power of the billionaire-owned mainstream media. It is both frightening and bewildering to witness the Niagara Falls of lies, slurs, deceitful commentaries and outrageous contortions of words to serve up the narrative that the champions of peace, tolerance and humanity are actually dyed-in-the-wool anti-Semites who represent a threat to the very existence of the Jewish community. Anyone with a fibre of independent thought is intuitively suspicious of such a ridiculous characterisation of socialists with track records in the movement of the likes of Corbyn, Livingstone and Williamson.

This book provides the context to the rabid and outrageous attacks on these men and thousands of others who dare to point out the criminality, brutality and immorality at the heart of Israel's apartheid state treatment of Palestine and the Palestinian people. Don't believe the rancid hype spewed by those in the payroll of the Israeli lobby and determined to use anti-Semitic slurs as a weapon against supporters of fundamental social change and progress. The weaponisation of anti-Semitism against Corbyn, Livingstone, Williamson and others is about defending the status quo, the rich and the powerful, the heinously unfair distribution of wealth and power in society. Those who challenge that status quo must be destroyed by the vicious media attack dogs and the pliable puppets within the Labour Party.

After reading this book you will be armed with the arguments to refute categorically the wholly untrue and unsavoury narrative pushed to the fore by the tiny cabal at the top of society. Read it and encourage others to do so and discuss it widely. Being a socialist and anti-Semite is incompatible. Being supportive of the Palestinian cause and right to exist does not make you anti-Semitic - it makes you human and an advocate of the rule of law and human rights.

Preface

For a book that will be concerning itself with the terms 'anti-Semitism' and 'Zionism' - words which, unfortunately, have become fraught in recent years - I think it important that I make it clear from the outset exactly what my intent shall be with their use.

Let us take each in turn. Using my dictionary, I find the following definition:

anti-Semitism

noun hostility to or prejudice against Jews.[1]

In brief, it will be this meaning, simple and readily understandable, that will be intended whenever this word is used throughout the pages that follow. For those that are interested, however, further discussion on this term, and the controversy it has evoked, might be useful for clarification at the outset.

The term 'anti-Semitism' is of relatively recent origins being first popularised by Wilhelm Marr in 1879 in his essay *"Der Weg zum Siege des Germanenthums uber das Judenthum"* (The Way to Victory of Germanicism over Judaism). Marr, who also founded the League of Anti-Semites in 1879, used the term "Antisemitismus" – hatred of the Jewish race instead of "Judenhass" – hatred of Jews.[2]

Marr's purpose was to posit the conflict between Germans and Jews as a racial, not a religious one. Indeed, it is of interest that the term is still used at all as, in the modern context, use of the term 'Semite' to mean a set of languages or ethnicity is not one that would be widely accepted today. In the nineteenth century, however, according to Professor Jonathan Judaken of Rhodes College:

"…anthropologists, philosophers, and Orientalists not only opposed 'Semitic' to 'Aryan' languages, they also maintained that languages encapsulated the indelible racial spirit of the people who used them. Both Jews and Arabs were implicated by the construct 'Semites'".[3]

Consequently, to use the phrase 'anti-Semitism' today is to, in some respect, recognise the historical reality that existed for centuries of both Jews and Arabs being considered under the same 'Semite' terminology. As Professor Gil Anidjar of Colombia University maintains:

"European self-constructions long depended upon a two-headed hydra: the Jew as the internal enemy, the theological enemy, and the Saracen, the Moor, the Arab, the Muslim, the Turk, or Islam itself as differing names that served as the external enemy, the political enemy".[4]

Recently, there has been a movement that argues that because 'Semite' is a term without any modern meaning, the hyphenated 'anti-Semitism' should be replaced by 'antisemitism'. However, as Professor Judaken explains:

"To hyphenate 'anti-Semitism' *consciously* today […] is to point to the forgotten intersections and interactions between Jews and Muslims, while remarking upon the history of the myth of "the Semite" that underpins the origins of the term. […] The choice to hyphenate is particularly significant in a political frame where Jews and Muslims are often figured as perpetual enemies despite the historical scholarship that shows otherwise".[5]

It will be this hyphenated form that I shall be using.[6] The very modern unhyphenated 'antisemitism' risks taking the term out of its historical context and, wittingly or unwittingly, more easily allows a form of historical amnesia of the long and strong connections between the Islamic/Arab world and the Jewish one.

A further discussion can be had on whether the term should continue to be used at all. For, as we will see in this book, it can be argued that its usage as a specious, ill-defined, catch-all term for everything from stereotypes to mass murder renders it increasingly meaningless. Perhaps, some scholars argue, given this situation, the term

Judeophobia should be more widely utilised to better articulate the disparate manifestations of anti-Jewish prejudices, suspicions, discrimination, persecution and hatred.

As Judaken notes: "...ancient Judeophobia [...] was characterised by important contextual differences from the early Christian Judeophobia of the Adversus Judaeos tradition. This anti-Judaism was transformed by the era of the Crusades and the High Medieval period, when [...] new fantasies about Jews [...] emerged. Modern racism developed out of the theological heritage of the Spanish Inquisition, the conquest of the Americas, transatlantic slavery, Enlightenment systems of categorisation, and the rise of nationalism in the wake of Napoleon. Post-Holocaust Judeophobia has taken new forms in a postcolonial era defined by globalisation".[7]

The use of 'Judeophobia" might also allow for a more nuanced discussion over the conflation that usually, and arguably unhelpfully, happens between the terms 'anti-Semitism' and 'racism' (for, it can be argued, the Jewish community in recent decades in Britain is not a 'race', nor does it see itself as racialised).

That said, for consistency, and because the term has been so widely appropriated and used in the context which I will be discussing in this book, it will be the hyphenated 'anti-Semitism' that I will commonly use.

The other highly charged word that will be in common usage throughout this book is Zionism. Again, if I refer to my dictionary, I find the following:

Zionism

noun a movement for the development of a Jewish nation in Israel.[8]

For the reader in a hurry to move on to the first chapter, this meaning will be sufficient to avoid confusion or misunderstanding. Again though, given the fraught modern context where even the definition of words is fought over, further discussion might be illuminating.

The term itself is derived from the word 'Zion' (Hebrew: צִיּוֹן, *Tzi-yon*), referring to Jerusalem. It arose in Eastern Europe in the nineteenth century to refer to the national resettlement of the Jews in, according to those who argued for it, their homeland, as well as the revitalisation and cultivation of the Hebrew language. It was, from its origins, undeniably colonialist.

It was this Zionist vision - the recreation of a Biblically-ordained homeland for the Jewish people - that was to endure and inform the creation of a Jewish state in Palestine at the expense of the native population, achieving its first significant success with the Balfour Declaration of 1917. Twenty years later, in 1937, the Peel Commission had proposed a plan to partition Palestine. In the eyes of then Jewish leader David Ben-Gurion, this would result in "a stepping stone to some further expansion and the eventual takeover of the whole of Palestine".[9] Ben-Gurion was only prepared to accept this partitioned state "on the basis that after we build a strong force following the establishment of the state, we will abolish the partition of the country and we will expand to the whole land of Israel".[10] The council of The Jewish Agency for Israel responded to the Peel Commission by stating that the transfer of Palestinian Arabs would be achieved not "by preaching 'sermons on the mount' but by machine-guns".[11]

The modern reader, operating in the shadow of the knowledge of the Holocaust, should not be blind to this reality, for it was explicit and widely acknowledged. In the words of one Labour Party annual conference motion in 1944:

"There is neither hope nor meaning in a 'Jewish National Home' unless, we are prepared to let Jews, if they wish, enter this tiny land [Palestine] in such numbers as to become a majority. There was a strong case for this before the war. There is an irresistible case now, after the unspeakable atrocities of the cold and calculated German Nazi plan to kill all Jews in Europe. Here, too, in Palestine surely is a case, on human grounds and to promote a stable settlement, for transfer of population. *Let the Arabs be encouraged to move out as the Jews move in* ".[12]

So, to make it clear, it will be the dictionary definition of 'Zionism' and 'Zionist' that is intended throughout this book. This meaning will also be informed by the historical context of the term – a Zionist being, at its inception, a term to describe someone who worked for the colonial occupation of lands that did not belong to them; Palestine, in other words.

Introduction

On the night of 27th June 2019, there was only one story in town - the 'disastrous' decision to readmit the Labour MP for Derby North, Chris Williamson, back into the party. "Williamson's readmission to Labour", Michael Segalov asserted in a prominent *Guardian* opinion piece, "isn't just an insult to the Jewish community, but to the entire party".[13] More than 150 Labour MPs signed a letter admitting to "hurt and anger" at the party's decision. Tom Watson, then Labour's deputy leader, claimed to be totally "bewildered by the decision".[14] The Board of Deputies of British Jews went further, calling it an "utter disgrace".[15] A Labour staff member, and organiser for the Jewish Labour Movement, was in no doubt that Williamson "has a pattern of antisemitic behaviour and his presence has created an environment where we are made unwelcome at work". Predictably, for those who had been following this story from the start, the harshest criticism was given by the Jewish Labour MP, Dame Margaret Hodge, who branded the move "appalling, outrageous and unacceptable".[16]

Those with only a passing interest in politics could be forgiven for taking this story at face value. For the coverage of this story was overwhelmingly one-sided and, despite the odd fringe voice, tended to merely repeat the voices yelling in outrage. Tom Watson, dependable as always to snipe and undermine from the Labour right, penned that it was "hard to overstate the depth of anger and hurt" caused by Chris Williamson's readmission.[16]

For others, however - those who, having the time or inclination to dig further, found little to cause such indignation and outrage - there was another possible explanation. An explanation involving the shameless politicking of the enemies of the newly-ascendant Labour left who, in finding allies in an avowedly pro-Israeli Zionist right, were able to harness and use the mass media seemingly at will to make their one-sided case.

That the chosen victim for this alliance was to be Chris Williamson was to prove disastrous for his political career in the Labour Party which had been his life. The lifelong socialist, forced out of the Labour Party, ultimately chose to contest his seat as an independent; the result, in as politically tribal a country as Britain, was never in doubt. Chris Williamson convincingly lost his seat, and his mainstream political career was over.

How had this come to pass? What heinous crimes was Chris Williamson guilty of? And, more widely, how can the media pick up a false story and - through constant repetition and amplification – permit these untruths, themselves, to become the main narrative? In many ways, it will be that nebulous quality 'truth' that will be the topic of this book.

"The most perfidious way of harming a cause consists of defending it deliberately with faulty arguments."

The Gay Science, Nietzsche

1 - The Manufactured anti-Semitism 'Crisis'

That Jews have suffered over the last two thousand years or so is beyond argument. The history of a 'people' without the security of a nation-state has left them exposed, for a variety of reasons, to persecution and ill-treatment. The current diaspora of the Jewish population, in itself very much a shadow of what it was before the formation of the modern state of Israel, is one of the consequences of that.

It is widely accepted that it was with the emergence and – over time - the dominance of Christianity in Europe, that worsened the situation for Jews. Somewhat paradoxically, given the fact that Jesus himself was Jewish, in some readings of Christianity, Judaism (and by extension, Jews themselves) can be seen as the enemy; that which Jesus had to fight in trying to establish his nascent new belief and those who, in this reading, ultimately murdered him. The theory of deicide, the apportioning of collective blame regarding the killing of the saviour, to all of the Jewish people, was to go on to enable anti-Semitism in the Christian world for millennia.

The history of what followed, the story of the 'wandering Jew', scattered around Europe (and elsewhere), often in sizeable numbers but rarely in such concentration and strength to afford real security, left them exposed. Who would one blame when the crops failed? When the economy crashed? It is always much easier to blame the minority.

Whether this history amounts to what is sometimes called, as Owen Jones states in his recent book, a "collective trauma" that informs the actions and thoughts of individual Jews today is more doubtful.[17] This is an important point to make because it is this alleged 'trauma' that is sometimes used to excuse the crimes of modern Israel in a way unthinkable for other countries. And, it should be noted, this 'trauma', the bloody pogroms and atrocities of the Jewish past are now, undeniably, history. With the exception of the Holocaust (and that occurrence is felt and remembered only through a handful of survivors and their recollections), there is no recent, direct experience of any atrocity for a Jew living in Britain today. Given this, given the contemporary context for the British Jewish experience, whilst being mindful of the sensitivities of history, one should also not allow oneself to backread the modern Israeli and Jewish experience through this interpretation of history – the Jew as the 'eternal' victim – alone.

Indeed, it is this argument - that because of a millennia-long history of victimhood, Jewish people will always be vulnerable until they settle on colonised (and stolen Palestinian) land - that Zionists continue to use shamelessly to further their argument that whatever Israel did, or does, is *necessary*. Stoking fear serves and furthers the Zionist cause. It is an understanding of this that will explain a lot of what has happened in the Labour Party in recent years.

In the modern context, the issue of anti-Semitism is inseparable from the Holocaust and, intrinsically connected to this, the founding of the modern state of Israel in 1948. And, in its early days, Israel could count on extensive support from all sectors of society, including the left. In the shadow of the Holocaust, it seemed to many that there was an incontestable need for a Jewish homeland to prevent such an atrocity from happening again. And, in its early days, with the pioneering kibbutzniks, the state's founders blended much of their Zionism with rhetoric that, at times, implied it was informed by socialism.[18]

Moreover, it is true that the state of Israel itself changed. Whilst it had been - at its very inception - a state that was founded on military might strong enough to be able to take and hold the land forcibly from the Palestinians, this had, on occasions, been leavened with left, egalitarian views e.g. the kibbutz movement. Over the decades that followed, these always-embattled liberal values were increasingly sidelined by the outright militarism and ugly ethnic nationalism that had been present from the nation's birth. By the 1980s, it would be hard for anyone on the left to ignore the plight of the Palestinians living among a regional military superpower in possession of the atomic bomb. In the intifadas that ensued, it would be a rare figure on the left who didn't automatically sympathise with the stone-throwing Palestinian rather than the machine gun-toting Israeli.

The anti-Semitism that is the principal concern of this book, however - one that is seen as a peculiar issue for the Labour Party - is a relatively recent phenomenon. One looks in vain for it as a live political issue amongst the British Jewish community or anywhere for that matter, prior to the last decade. So, what occurred during this time that resulted in this claim becoming such an alleged issue that some individuals and groups actually talked of British Jews having to physically flee the country if the Labour Party achieved power?[19]

Labour MP Michael Dugher - at the time of his comments in 2015, vice-chair of the influential Labour Friends of Israel group - saw the problem arising with the Ed Miliband leadership forcing through the whip, a motion backing Palestinian statehood in 2014. Echoing apparently concerned commentators in the years to follow, he stated: "Too many people in the Jewish community felt that Labour wasn't their party anymore". The Labour Party, Dugher opined, should be "more proud of our ties with Israel" and "give credit for the extraordinary achievement that the state of Israel has had".[20]

Other modern commentators, keen to decry Labour's alleged anti-Semitism, point to different incidents; incidents that often went unnoticed at the time. One of these relatively obscure events that proceeded to have massive ramifications occurred on 3rd March 2009 when Jeremy Corbyn, then a relatively unheralded backbencher, stated, in a speech at a Stop the War coalition meeting, that it would be his "pleasure" to welcome his "friends" from Hamas and Hezbollah.[21]

For many on the left, there was - and remains - nothing wrong in this. As a long-standing veteran of various peace initiatives and lifelong internationalist, Corbyn involving himself in a movement seeking peace and de-escalation in the Middle East should come as no surprise.

For a politician also to use, in passing, such everyday diplomatic language as 'friends' is, to be frank, just the diurnal reality of politics; to be a diplomat often necessitates the couching of ones language in such politesse.

Indeed, one can look through the long history of politics to see individuals using ameliorating language when necessary. Did Corbyn's use of 'friends' mean that he supported every word and action of Hamas and Hezbollah? Of course not. That would be as ludicrous as believing that, when Conservative prime minister Theresa May sent Martin McGuinness her "best wishes", it meant she supported the IRA mainland bombing campaign.[22]

Corbyn indeed, sensitive as he always was to causing upset, was to later state: "It was inclusive language I used which with hindsight I would rather not have used".[23] All perfectly reasonable. However, as so often is the case, the damage had already been done. Corbyn would forever, on social media, be dogged by these words by opponents only bent on criticism rather than understanding.

Similarly, in the same speech, when he announced that "we are opposed to Zionism", that would be a simple, unarguable statement of fact held by the majority of the left in Britain.[21] Again, it would go on to be quoted time and time again in the future by those wishing, often for their own narrow reasons, to label the new leader of the Labour Party, and the wider left in general, as anti-Semitic.

Indeed, it is remarkable that the pro-Israeli lobby has managed to turn this opposition to Zionism into a contentious issue. For why should anyone on the left automatically agree with the continuing forcible occupation of Palestinian lands by Israel? It is, of course, always possible, with Israel unique amongst modern nations in defining itself in terms of a religion (one cannot be Israeli and be a Sikh, for example, in the same way that you could combine nationhood and faith in just about every other country on earth – Judaism is bound into this nationhood inseparably), that a few members of the left would confuse criticism of the Israeli state with criticism of the Jew. Indeed, it is an understandable mistake, given that the two terms in many contexts could be interchangeable. For one would know (or strongly suspect – there remains, of course, always, the oft-invisible presence of the Israeli Arab), with a certainty impossible with any other nation, that an Israeli Olympic athlete would also be Jewish.

This attempt to render any criticism of Zionism taboo would, if successful, in one fell swoop, shut down much of the criticism of modern Israel. What better way to do this than to convince people that criticism of Zionism is not only anti-Israel, it is also anti-Semitic? For the Israeli Zionists and 'Netanyahus', who came to dominate their domestic politics both at home and on the international stage, this would be a very convenient way of defusing any criticism.

In 2009 this was still, for the most part, all to come. In later years though, in article after article alluding to the Labour Party's anti-Semitism, they nearly all referred back to this speech. The *Daily Mail* and others simply wouldn't let it go. This incident (and others) became part of the familiar zombie arguments of the online age, and even if repudiated or refuted, they would consistently and anaemically resurface. For many on the political right and elsewhere, it simply became habitual to refer to Corbyn as someone who loved Hamas, who loved terrorists, and hated Jews. Such was the frightening world of British politics in the social media age.

Interestingly though, at the time, Corbyn's comments received little to no scrutiny. It wasn't until years later, on the 18th July 2015, that *Daily Telegraph* journalist Andrew Gilligan, in perhaps the first newspaper article to seize upon this incident, directly linked Corbyn's comments to anti-Semitism.[24] From that point on, from Corbyn's insurgency to his victory and eventual defeat, the references to that one speech in 2009 were to become so commonplace as to be enshrined or accepted as fact. It has become a psychological truism that if one repeats a lie often enough, it becomes the truth. Rarely has such a process been so dramatically accomplished than with Labour's anti-Semitism wars.

A short time after Gilligan's piece in the *Telegraph* referencing Corbyn's Stop the War speech, the *Daily Mail* headlines screamed about Corbyn's "long standing" links with "notorious" Holocaust denier and anti-Semite Paul Eisen.[25] The truth, as always, was far more mundane. Corbyn, as a long-standing campaigner for Palestinian rights, had attended a handful of meetings for the group Eisen was connected with, namely Deir Yassin Remembered. As a group that ostensibly existed to remember the undisputed massacre of Palestinian villagers in 1948, Jeremy's involvement was not surprising. When the *Daily Mail* approached him for a comment on this connection, his office simply stated that: "Paul Eisen is not someone Jeremy Corbyn's office has any dealings with....anyone can call themselves a 'long-time associate' when in fact this is not the case. Paul Eisen clearly holds some of the most extreme views and Jeremy totally opposes them and disassociates himself from them".[25]

Case over, one might think. Except it wasn't. These stories now began to set the template for any mischievous journalist with an axe to grind. And as the newspaper column inches mounted, for the more passive follower of politics, even if one was not to draw any conclusion oneself, to keep seeing Corbyn and the left linked to anti-Semitism in this way could only be damaging.

Perhaps at this point, if there had been a rebuttal or fight back from Corbyn or the parliamentary Labour left, things might have been different. But there was no organised resistance, no lawsuits filed. Time and again, Labour MPs only mouthed their (obvious) opposition to anti-Semitism and ignored what was really happening - an orchestrated smear campaign - for fear, one can assume, that tackling the issue would be painful. One is reminded of the patient suffering symptoms, afraid to go to the doctor for fear of what they might say, so puts off appointment after appointment while, steadily, the symptoms get worse.

Consequently, the *Daily Mail* and others (soon to notably include *The Guardian*) were to learn that, on this issue, they would always be given an open goal. They could make an allegation, gain negative headlines, damage the party, all with little effort or Labour defence.

So many of these false, misleading, but very widely covered stories were to emerge in such a short space of time linking Labour to anti-Semitism that a book intending to analyse every single story in detail would run the risk of becoming bogged down in mind-numbing perplexity. Which is, of course, the aim of such allegations – to simply bully the victim, and the reader, into stoical acceptance. It is only the rare reader with the time and inclination to be able to delve further into the story that is able to establish the tenuousness of most of these claims. The 'truth' though was increasingly irrelevant, and it was typically invisible, crowded out from the public space by the sheer scale of the coverage and level of vitriol.

These attack articles on Corbyn and the left hadn't come from nowhere though; there was previous form. And perhaps the first instance that had come to the wider public's attention, with Labour linked to anti-Semitism in such an open way, was the case of Ken Livingstone.

In February 2005, whilst leaving a City Hall LGBT reception, Livingstone objected to an *Evening Standard* journalist photographer "harassing" other guests, with Livingstone going on to ask if he had been a "German war criminal". When the journalist in question, Oliver Finegold, replied that he was Jewish, Livingstone replied: "Well, you might be, but actually you are just like a concentration camp guard. You're just doing it 'cause you're paid to, aren't you?"[26]

What is one to say about this incident? It is definitely unfortunate that a relatively minor fracas with the paparazzi (Livingstone was annoyed at what he saw as harassment at an LGBT event by a Conservative-leaning newspaper journalist) would result in allusions to the Holocaust, more so if one of the parties happened to be Jewish. But what one could definitely not say, and what the Board of Deputies of British Jews (BoD) would do, in a move that would become very familiar to Labour members, is state that Livingstone's remarks were anti-Semitic.

That it is obvious there is nothing in these comments which implies discriminatory or unfair treatment towards Jewish people should go without saying. For some reason, the Labour Party seemed peculiarly reticent in admitting this, preferring the narrative that Livingstone's comments betrayed a skulking hatred of the Jew.

The muddle-headedness shown here and timidity to call out something blatantly false, seems to come from the worldwide, generational fallout following the Second World War. The horror of the Holocaust has long been an unchallenged fixture in the British education system and the modern political world, and rightfully so. And if a long-standing body like the BoD were to call someone out as anti-Semitic, it would seem difficult, or at least awkward, for a gentile to challenge this in any way, for there is an undeniable authority that comes from being a member of the group allegedly being mistreated. It would seem fair to say, for example, that the views of a black boy from a Peckham estate on racism would be seen as more insightful than a white woman's view from a Home Counties village. Or a woman's opinion on male chauvinism compared to that of a man's.

However, for this bias of belief to work, it relies on all parties acting in good faith i.e. their alleged grievances being genuinely held ones. Problems arise if an individual or group, for reasons of their own, decide to act or speak dishonestly.

It remains the case that few individuals with any political clout have felt emboldened enough to challenge the BoD on its views. Interestingly, perhaps the fiercest resistance has come from within the Jewish community itself.

The BoD's origins date back to 1760, but, strangely, throughout this period of British history, its thoughts lay dormant. It is only recently, in its wranglings with the British Labour Party, that it has come to any prominence. One searches fruitlessly for its role in, say, combatting the *real* anti-Semitism of the 1930s and 1970s, where the left, as always, was notable for forming the large bulk of resistance. BoD's role, as the self-appointed voice of the Jewish community, is something of an irritant for many of the Jewish community, appalled that any modern complex social group, with a multiplicity of views, can be co-opted by such a monolithic organisation.

A younger organisation, the Jewish Voice for Labour (JVL), has been strident in its criticism. Delivering a list of 'demands' on 12th March 2020 to the organisation, they state, quite bluntly, that "The Board of Deputies [of British Jews] (BoD) claims to speak for a British 'Jewish community' but they represent only a minority of Jews and do not represent us." Indeed, they continue: to claim that there is "a single Jewish community who share the views of the BoD is discriminatory".[27]

It is a source of much frustration that, given the unrepresentative makeup of its members, given the biased and overt nature of its politics, when the media require an opinion from the 'Jews' (which the JVL point out is, at best, problematic) they invariably reach for the BoD. And without fail, the BoD has seized this opportunity to attack Labour and encourage, at every turn, the conflation of criticism of Israel with criticism of the Jewish people.

Ken Livingstone, in this regard, was clearly a marked man by the BoD. The attacks intensified when, in a BBC Radio London interview with Vanessa Feltz (in April 2016), he said: "When Hitler won his election in 1932 his policy then was that Jews should be moved to Israel. He was supporting Zionism before he went mad and ended up killing six million Jews".[28]

It could be argued that Livingstone should have articulated this historical observation differently. Wording it the way he did, perhaps, gave the smear merchants an excuse to express faux outrage that Livingstone had somehow suggested that Hitler was acting reasonably "before he went mad". But, to label his comments 'anti-Semitic' was absurd. Livingstone clearly stated that Hitler murdered six million Jews. This is no deranged Holocaust denier. The comment that prompted such ire was that Hitler "was supporting Zionism"[28] to solve his 'Jewish problem', even though it is a valid historical observation which Livingstone is surely entitled to cite. (Interested parties should refer to the Haavara Agreement[29] between Nazi Germany and Zionist German Jews for more on this.)

In what was to become familiar to Labour Party watchers, the usual suspects lined up to take potshots. Labour MP John Mann outrageously claimed that Livingstone was a "Nazi apologist".[30] Tom Watson said Livingstone's comments were "vile".[31] The decision was eventually left to Ken Livingstone, who, as befitting a giant of the party - one who had been a pivotal part of its modern history - thought it would be distracting to remain as a member. So, on the 21st May 2018, after years of criticism from the political party he had given his life to, he resigned. What a shameful moment for the Labour Party that such a historical figure should be forced to depart under a false cacophony of allegations of anti-Semitism. One would hope, at some point, he receives the recognition and apology that he deserves.

Perhaps the nadir of the hyperbole from within the Jewish community came from the much-reported joint editorial of the *Jewish Chronicle*, *Jewish News* and *Jewish Telegraph*, on 26th July 2018. Amongst a tirade of criticism, they stated that an "existential threat to Jewish life in this country would be posed by a Jeremy Corbyn led government".[32]

It is worth pausing over this remark. An 'existential' threat? A threat to the very existence of Jews in this country?! An outside observer, if shown these words, unaware of the wider context, may conclude that they must have been written following the aftermath of a bloody pogrom, or a Kristallnacht. Or, at least some organised and open anti-Jewish movement pledging itself to the removal of the Jews from the UK.

Of course, there was none of this. And who was being accused? A Labour Party whose members, from the dark days of the 1930s to the street fighting of the 1970s, had battled - often literally - side by side with the Jewish community in defence of their rights.

It was a ludicrous assertion. But how did Labour MP Joan Ryan respond to these attacks? By rebutting them? By pointing out Corbyn's impeccable record on this issue?[33] Unfortunately not. A Labour government would be, she alleged with absolutely no evidence, "an existential threat to the community".[34] With friends like these indeed.

One can speculate on this hyperbole. If one suspends one's incredulity for a moment, then perhaps it was conceivable there were some people among the ranks of Labour MPs and members of the BoD who were genuinely alarmed at the prospect of a Labour government. Maybe they believed that through Corbyn using the word 'friends' as a seemingly affectionate reference to Hamas and Hezbollah, that what he really meant was there would soon be a Labour-led physical attack on the denizens of Golders Green.

But returning to reality - if that hypothetical flight of fancy isn't the case, if the majority don't believe that Corbyn would, on the first day of his Labour Party's new governance, unleash an anti-Jewish pogrom, then what is one to make of such remarks?

Watching Labour throughout this time has been a constant exercise in surprise. Just when one thought the limit of overstatement and hysteria had been reached, the following day a new low would be set. For example, in August 2018, in an interview with the *New Statesman*, the media's favourite rabbi, Jonathan Sacks, had absolutely no compunction in using the bluntest of language, openly calling Corbyn "an anti-Semite".[35]

He saved his most hyperbolic reaction though, to comment upon an obscure Corbyn speech that had recently been exhumed by forces motivated to damage Jeremy and the party (who had, presumably, spent hours trawling the internet for such things). In this speech, dug up from 2013, Corbyn addressed a 'Palestinian return' meeting and accused some "Zionists" of lacking an "understanding" of "English irony".[36] For Sacks, though, this wasn't an example of sensitive phraseology by an MP who has spoken millions of words in the public eye, it was an example of "the most offensive statement made by a senior British politician since Enoch Powell's 1968 'Rivers of Blood' speech". Sacks, not content with this balderdash, persisted: "It was divisive, hateful and, like Powell's speech it undermines the existence of an entire group of British citizens by depicting them as essentially alien......[When] he implies...Jews are not fully British, he is using the language of classic pre-war European anti-Semitism".[35]

The mind boggles. There comes a point on this issue, when the divergence between words spoken and what is being alleged by the various bad-faith actors, is so vast that it defies analysis. One is stunned that such a leading figure could make such a ridiculous leap, comparing Corbyn's words to the language of the Nazis and the malign right. Indulging in the most alarmist and frankly disrespectful comments towards the memory of the *real* victims of anti-Semitism, Sacks should have been laughed out of the interview. Predictably he wasn't. In a stark dereliction of duty, the media duly listened to his words and then went on to repeat them as serious commentary meriting discussion.

Perhaps, over time, given the lack of evidence in relation to these baseless assertions, the sheer ridiculousness of them would have brought the whole witch-hunt to a crashing halt. There came to be an issue though that many proponents of the witch-hunt considered a matter of fact - something of substance they could pin their allegations around. That issue was to be the IHRA's 'working definition' of anti-Semitism.

On 26th May 2016, the IHRA, or the International Holocaust Remembrance Alliance to give it its full title, adopted the working definition of anti-Semitism - drawn up, but never adopted, by the European Monitoring Centre on Racism and Xenophobia 13 years earlier.

This refers to "a certain perception of Jews, which may be expressed as hatred towards Jews. Rhetorical and physical manifestations of antisemitism are directed toward Jewish or non-Jewish individuals and/or their property, towards Jewish community institutions and religious facilities".[37]

It is doubtful that many would find this contentious. One might inquire as to whether there was a need to define a term that seemed to have been perfectly well understood and used for a long time. The Oxford English Dictionary, for instance, defines anti-Semitism simply as "Hostility to or prejudice against Jews".[1] This definition patently works and is straightforward and clear. And when one considers the complications that arise from the IHRA's much lengthier attempt, it is hard not to accept that it is preferable. For much vagueness exists with the IHRA definition. For example, the use of 'may' in the phrasing, "...which may be expressed as hatred towards Jews", is interesting.[38] For if that is the case, one asks, what does anti-Semitism look like when it isn't expressed through hatred towards Jews? We aren't told.

Several senior lawyers certainly weren't impressed. Hugh Tomlinson QC described it as "unclear and confusing" and said it "should be used with caution".[38] In Sir Stephen Sedley's view, it "fails the first test of any definition: it is indefinite".[39] Sir Geoffrey Bindman wrote: "Unfortunately, the definition and the examples are poorly drafted [and] misleading".[40] And Geoffrey Robertson concluded, "It is imprecise, confusing and open to misinterpretation and even manipulation".[41]

Given that the new anti-Semitism 'definition' from the IHRA seemed to be more problematic and flawed than its predecessor, one might ask why there was a need for it in the first place. Where was the demand for further 'clarification' when it caused such obfuscation? It was only relatively recently that the term engendered or gave rise to any controversy. The previous consensus defining anti-Semitism's components had broken down due to the ongoing Israeli/Palestinian issue, and to what extent criticism of Israel was valid, and at what point that became anti-Semitism.

When this occurred, when critics on the Zionist right - seeking a definition of a 'new anti-Semitism' - became prominent, this allowed the politicisation of the issue; the fallout from which, it could be argued, the Labour Party is dealing with today.

What was the 'new anti-Semitism' lobby? It was expressed clearly by Irwin Cotler, a Canadian human rights law professor who summed it up in 2010 thus: "In a word [sic], classical anti-Semitism is the discrimination against, denial of, or assault upon the rights of Jews to live as equal members of whatever society they inhabit. The new anti-Semitism involves the discrimination against, denial of, or assault upon the right of the Jewish people to live as an equal member of the family of nations, with Israel as the targeted 'collective Jew among the nations'".[42]

For Zionists then, this new definition - to be able to call someone an anti-Semite for disputing the legitimacy of Israel - would be a perfect way to shut down any debate before it had even started.

From the outset, it was never subjected to full scrutiny with only a handful of people signing off on the initial draft. And, ironically perhaps, for those like Corbyn and Chris Williamson, passionately committed to fighting real anti-Semitism, this new 'definition' made the job harder, not easier. For if anti-Semitism is conflated with criticism of Israel, which this definition allows, then it only serves to cloud and confuse.

From the moment the IHRA started pushing bodies to accept this definition, there were problems. The main contention arose when the IHRA went on to list examples of what might be seen specifically as instances of anti-Semitism. That it felt the need to provide examples seems unusual. It can be argued this emanated from its initial, hazy wording. Surely any decent, clear definition wouldn't need to give examples. In spite of this, some examples were straightforward, but a few were controversial from the outset...

"Denying the Jewish people their right to self-determination, e.g., by claiming that the existence of a State of Israel is a racist endeavour".[43]

For many on the left, this seemed odd. For, it was argued, it seemed self-evident that the state of Israel was a racist institution from its inception. Where else, in the post-war world, could a nation-state define itself so exclusively in terms of identity? The apartheid state of South Africa, perhaps? Surely modern Israel, quite openly giving preferential treatment to the worldwide Jewish community, is a similar case.

Now, one might disagree with this view, arguing that not giving sufficient prominence to the historical context is ultimately unfair. It is an entirely different thing though, to deny people the right to make comparisons (even if you think they are wrong) for fear of them being harshly and ruinously labelled anti-Semites.

Other examples caused problems too:

"Drawing comparisons of contemporary Israeli policy to that of the Nazis".[43]

Again, this would seem an odd and unnecessary thing to include, as many *did* think it was fair to draw a comparison between the treatment of the Palestinians in the West Bank and especially Gaza and the persecutory Nazi regime. One might think it wrong and needlessly divisive, given the history, to make this comparison or consider it best advised to make one's case without trying to draw such parallels, ladened as they are with emotional baggage. But what should not be countenanced is denying someone the *right* to make such a connection, thus pretending that the modern Israeli state is somehow ahistorical. And whatever one's thoughts, linking or making synonymous the contemporary acts of the state of Israel with the acts of the Nazis does not demonstrate 'hostility or prejudice towards Jews', just as comparisons between the Khmer Rouge and the Nazis does not indicate hostility towards Khmers.

One can go on. A further example stated that it would be anti-Semitic to "accuse Jewish people of being more loyal to Israel than the country they live in".[43] Well, of course, it could be! But just as likely, this could be a mere statement of fact, for there surely exist Jewish people whose primary loyalty *is* to the state of Israel over their home nation. Why the need to turn such a statement into an anti-Semitic one? One can only conclude that it was *another* attempt to stifle criticism of Israel.

These many and various problems notwithstanding, the IHRA's creaking and discordant 'definition' eventually landed in the in-tray of Labour's NEC. On 5th July 2018, it formally embraced the 38-word 'working definition' of anti-Semitism. It also accepted seven of the examples and, indeed, added two more. So far, so good, one might think. However, merely by questioning four of the examples, and by suggesting a change of language with the aim of protecting freedom of speech and simplifying the disciplinary process, the issue fulminated in a blaze of controversy.[44]

The Parliamentary Labour Party (PLP), as usual reserving its militancy and organisational skills to undermine Corbyn's leadership rather than the Conservatives, voted "overwhelmingly" for the full IHRA definition to be adopted. The Labour MP, Wes Streeting, described the Labour leadership's refusal to fall into total obeisance before this new code as "utterly contemptible".[45] Keir Starmer, on the influential Andrew Marr show, said "I urge everybody within the Labour Party to listen to the voices that have come out in recent days and get to a position where we are supporting the full definition".[46] As was to happen so often, there seemed to be little to no willingness on behalf of any of these serial complainants to actually consider with any seriousness the NEC's objections; just an overwhelming desire to roll over and acquiesce to any criticism, perceived or otherwise, from the media or certain sectors of the Jewish community. (The politics of a jellyfish rather than that of an independent and confident political party.)

The BoD professed total disbelief in the NEC's minor, academic quibbling over some of the points, stating it was "impossible to understand why Labour refuses to align itself with this universal definition".[47] True to form, BoD's playing loose and fast with the truth (suggesting that the new code had been 'universally' accepted) did not prevent such mendacity being embraced without question by the media at large and repeated parrot-fashion. In fact, the reality, in 2018, when this debate was raging, revealed that only six of the 31 countries that make up the IHRA, had formally adopted it.[48]

Interestingly, despite immense pressure to fall into line, many UK universities still refuse to adopt this flawed 'definition'- notwithstanding the outrageous intervention of the education secretary Gavin Williamson, who declared it "frankly disturbing"[49] that there were still institutions that wished to champion free speech![50] Prominent among these refuseniks was the University College London whose academic board soberly declared: "This specific working definition is not fit for purpose within a university setting and has no legal basis for enforcement".[51]

The Guardian, relishing its newly found role to undermine and attack the Corbyn leadership, stated that Labour's obstinacy showed a "sickness" in the party.[52]

Unfortunately, in what was becoming a familiar bugle call or pattern, the NEC, rather than argue their position, quickly rolled over in the face of the faux righteousness of the PLP and the media, by adopting the definition in full on the 4th September 2018.

Tellingly, Stephen Kinnock responded: "I don't personally think that now is the time to be putting in additions and qualifications. That's pouring more fuel on the fire, and that's the last thing we should be doing right now".[53] Most Labour MPs, rather than dealing with the issues at hand and getting to the truth of the matter, were more concerned with avoiding criticism.

As Jewish academic, Dr Brian Klug, observed: "I have not yet come across a critic of the NEC Code – I mean a critic who places a premium on combating antisemitism – who acknowledges [the points that significantly enhance the IHRA text], let alone welcomes them as the enhancements that they are. They are passed over in silence, as if the IHRA document were a sacred text whose words may not be tampered with – not even if the text can be improved".[54]

Only a very few MPs, notably Chris Williamson, seemed to show any interest in whether the definition was a good one or not. As he argued quite calmly in a talkRADIO interview, some of the examples "fetter free speech".[55]

As ever, Williamson's high-minded position was very much a minority view within the PLP, and the Labour Party's stance of acquiescence and passive surrender prevailed. Unsurprisingly, the feckless and dutiful argument articulated by Stephen Kinnock (to not concern oneself with what was right, only with what was popular), totally failed when it came to defusing criticism.

Perhaps this was because the critics of the party would never be satisfied. Joan Ryan, Labour MP and chair of the Labour Friends of Israel (LFI) group, at least did not mince her words: "Jeremy Corbyn appals me – and his behaviour will get no better....Nor should we pretend that even full acceptance of IHRA ends this battle against antisemitism in the Labour Party".[56] A member of the Jesuit order raging against the Protestants would have recognised these sentiments. Ryan and her ilk were engaged in a permanent war against the unbelievers where no concession would ever be enough.

The increasing disconnect between those mostly on the left (interested in having a rigorous discussion around the issue of anti-Semitism) and the majority on the right of the party together with the media at large (fixated with the political fallout of such arguments) was symptomatic of a wider, cynical plot. And it was this latter group who dominated the airwaves, and who, despite their crocodile tears, showed little interest in the subject itself aside from the flimsiest sentimental allegations.

Perhaps the final word on the IHRA fall out should go to the man who wrote it - Kenneth Stern. In 2004, as the American Jewish Committee's anti-Semitism expert, he was the lead drafter on the initial 'working definition' which came, as we have seen, to be the IHRA's. In a striking article written for *The Guardian* in December 2019, Stern pulls no punches. From 2010, he states, "right-wing Jewish groups took the 'working definition', which had some examples about Israel (such as holding Jews collectively responsible for the actions of Israel, and denying Jews the right to self-determination), and decided to weaponise it". It (and the examples included) was never intended to be a test to decide absolutely what was anti-Semitic or not, but merely something "created primarily so that European data collectors could know what to include and exclude". A way for anti-Semitism to be monitored.[57]

Unfortunately, in universities, political parties and nation-states, its simplistic wholesale adoption (along with all the examples) merely serves as an "attack on free speech". Stern makes no bones about it. He identifies as a Zionist. But in the best traditions of democracy, he sees it as fundamental that "anti-Zionists have the right to free expression".[57]

He concludes:

"Antisemitism is a real issue, but too often people, both on the political right and political left, give it a pass if a person has the 'right' view on Israel. Historically, antisemitism thrives best when leaders stoke the human capacity to define an 'us' and a 'them', and where the integrity of democratic institutions and norms (such as free speech) are under assault".[57]

> "If that the earth could teem with woman's tears,
> each drop she falls would prove a crocodile."
>
> *Othello,* Shakespeare

2 - The Strange Tale of Luciana Berger

Whilst considering the role of democracy in the Labour Party it is worth, perhaps, considering for a moment, the strange role of Luciana Berger – and how her story came to be seen, by the Parliamentary Labour Party (PLP) and the media, as the most toxic example of anti-Semitism in the party. In this narrative, Berger was portrayed as a young female MP who was subjected to constant abuse within the party simply because she was Jewish (ultimately leading to people being imprisoned for hate crimes), resulting in her having to flee the party for the sanctuary of another.

Tom Watson, never one to eschew hyperbole given the opportunity, said - in the pained and bewildered voice he affected for such interviews - that the Liverpool Wavertree MP being bullied out of "her own party by racist thugs... [was] the worst day of shame" in the Labour Party's 120-year history.[58]

This tale, that of a young female MP, subject to constant abuse within her own party simply because she was Jewish, has become one of those stories, like Corbyn calling Hamas 'friends', that is always returned to, always referred to, whenever anyone wants to list the alleged crimes of Labour and the left.

But there is another reading of this, another tale to be spun. It starts with familiarity. For Berger, followed in the well-trodden path of New Labour royalty. A privately educated president of the NUS, she was to be further ingratiated into the New Labour aristocratic set when she had a relationship with Tony Blair's son, Euan.

No surprise then, that in 2010, following a stint as the Director of Labour Friends of Israel (LFI), she was centrally imposed and parachuted into the safe Liverpool Wavertree constituency. Typically, this was done without any consultation with the local membership i.e. whether they wanted to be represented by someone with no previous knowledge of the area.

This lack of connection was made abundantly clear to the locals when the *Liverpool Echo* asked her about Merseyside football icon, Bill Shankly, to which Berger replied that she had never heard of him.[59] Taken in isolation, this might seem unfair, as not everyone is familiar with the Liverpool football legend of the 1960s and 1970s. Indeed, for someone of Berger's background, pre-existing knowledge of Shankly might even be surprising. The point is, though, that ignorance of this topic would be unthinkable for a local. A native candidate would know the history of such a working-class hero only too well and surely, therefore, make a better MP with all the richness that understanding an area entails.

For a candidate to be imposed on Liverpool in this way was problematic to many locals, and so, consequently, right from the start, the Berger issue was much more about local democracy than anti-Semitism.

Berger's lack of connections to the area caused predictable uproar amongst the locals. Ricky Tomlinson, a famous Liverpool actor with a history of trade union militancy, expressed such feelings quite clearly: "This woman that they have parachuted in from London could not even answer some easy questions about Liverpool. It reminds me of when Labour parachuted Shaun Woodward into St Helens". He went on: "People say if you want you could be letting the Tories in. But there is no difference between the Conservatives and New Labour".[60]

The issues of disconnection between the Labour Party and its traditional support - fervently displayed in the 2019 election with the newly branded 'Red Wall' largely decamping to the Tories - was evident much earlier to anyone who cared to look. At the time, though, just as it had for decades, the Labour Party seemed uninterested in these generational shifts and - even as the ground moved beneath it - was arrogant enough to believe that these seats were theirs indefinitely. Tomlinson bemoaned: "At one time, Liverpool had a contingent of working-class MPs....I just can't understand why they have picked someone from London. It just does not make sense to me".[60]

He wasn't the only one. Upon Berger successfully securing her position as Labour candidate for the Liverpool Wavertree seat, another local framed the problem very clearly. "Retired journalist John Hubble, 77, said he had been involved in socialist politics all his life but was considering drastic action to register his disgust. 'I will probably spoil my paper I feel so strongly. My wife feels the same. I don't take that decision frivolously. I know people who have died for democracy and I would as well.'"[61] One notes at this time, in 2010, the absence of commentary on anti-Semitism in connection to Luciana Berger. Later, however, displeasure of any kind expressed by a local, or Labour member, was framed entirely through the prism of bigotry and anti-Semitism. It is clear, though, that for John Hubble and Ricky Tomlinson, this was an issue *purely* about local democracy.

Still, despite the dissatisfaction that many local members felt, they were devoted to the success of the Labour Party and so campaigned successfully for Berger in 2010 and, after her victory in that election, again in 2015.

Discontent was brewing beneath the surface though. Berger, being a prominent member of the New Labour elite, was - like many in the PLP - not enamoured with the rise to power of Corbyn and the left. When, on the 27th June 2016, she resigned her position as shadow mental health minister, she was knowingly taking part in an organised mass resignation of shadow front benchers, aimed at undermining the democratically elected leader; one widely supported by local members. Predictably, this wasn't overly appreciated by her Constituency Labour Party (CLP), amongst whom Corbyn - as with the membership at large - was overwhelmingly popular. In a sign of the displeasure, one of the local members stated: "We would like her to come out publicly like other MPs have done and apologise for not supporting him in the past".[62]

Throughout this period, in Liverpool Wavertree, as with the rest of the country, it was the membership fighting a rear-guard action to save Corbyn from the undemocratic manoeuvrings of the PLP right.

These urgings by the local membership for their MP to at least acknowledge their right to choose their leader were not respected. In early 2018, after repeatedly failing to answer a question in a TV interview which asked whether she would be leaving Labour to form a new, centrist party, Berger's CLP invited her to attend a meeting where the following motion would be discussed: "Instead of fighting for a Labour government, our MP is continually using the media to criticise the man we all want to be prime minister". For Tom Watson, this attempt by the local membership to temper the ongoing destabilising actions of their local MP against their party and their leader wasn't a sign of robust democracy, however, but "the bullying hatred from members of her own local party".[63]

Those on the right were desperate to paint this as another example of anti-Semitism in the party, even when there was no evidence of it. As John McDonnell put it, it was merely the local party expressing concern over their MP as "it looks as though what has happened is Luciana has been in the media associated with a breakaway party and hasn't been clear that she rejects that".[63]

Labour MP after Labour MP, though, were more than happy to leap to the defence of this internal saboteur. Chris Leslie, erstwhile Labour MP for Nottingham East (and also a member of the select group of Labour MPs that would soon make their much-publicised departure from the Labour Party to join the very short-lived 'Change' political party), said: "I have never heard of such a ridiculous situation.... He [Corbyn] should never have allowed his allies to have gone after Luciana like that in the first place. I have a feeling they will realise this is a terrible, terrible judgement".[63]

And Chuka Umunna (another soon-to-be member of the nascent, new ex-Labour political group in a totally coincidental and non-coordinated act) also spoke up: "Are we going to act? Defend a colleague in the face of this outrage?"[63] Members might be forgiven for thinking that this staged outrage from Umunna and others would have been more appropriately expressed in relation to the false labelling of Labour members as bullies. Or worse, that it was a ruse to cover the continual, undemocratic, destabilising attacks by some in their own party.

At least this charade, unlike many others which were to fester inside the party while outwardly acting as a pretence of loyalty, eventually came out into the open. Despite being labelled as bullies the local membership was, in fact, absolutely correct. On the morning of Monday 18th February 2019, Luciana Berger, along with Leslie and Umunna, and others who leapt so passionately to her defence, left the party - the party (and seat) that the local activists and membership had campaigned so hard for Berger to win. And it would be they, the members, painted as the guilty party, tainted and taunted as bigots and racists, while the real plotters sailed off into the sunset. There was little reporting of the fact that her membership's fears and criticisms proved to be well founded.

Berger didn't hold back, of course. The problem wasn't her constant undermining of the democratically elected leadership, but rather that Labour was "institutionally antisemitic".[64]

It would seem odd for someone to say that about a party whose base had worked tirelessly on her behalf. It would also seem odd for someone to claim anti-Semitism when, to this day, there remains no evidence of any anti-Semitism directed at Berger from *within* the Liverpool Wavertree constituency or from anyone with any *serious* connections to the party. And perhaps it is to state the blindingly obvious but it would seem, again, odd for any genuine, institutionally anti-Semitic party to have actually campaigned for, and worked with for years, well, a Jew!

So where did the furore about anti-Semitism come from? That Berger, a prominent Jewish MP, was the victim of anti-Semitic abuse is undeniable. Between 2014 and 2018, four neo-Nazis were jailed for crimes against her, including anti-Semitic abuse and harassment.[65] But one has a hard time locating *any* evidence of maltreatment towards her that originated from within or close to the party. In a long, rambling article devoted to her complaints, the best Luciana Berger was able to come up with was her claim that "the abuse was regularly dismissed by Labour members in her Liverpool Wavertree constituency, who responded to her recollections by sitting stony-faced and suggesting that she should be more supportive of Jeremy Corbyn".[66]

It is true that she does, in the same article, recount some horrible, truly anti-Semitic things which she experienced. But, in none of this, is there a discernible connection to the Labour Party. Perhaps one should have some sympathy for someone who has been the victim of such abuse. Perhaps, one appreciates, it might affect your perspective if subjected to it. Perhaps one might even begin to see shades and caricatures of anti-Semites everywhere. Perhaps. And I have some sympathy with this view. But I have none with the journalists who, time after time, merely repeated and magnified her allegations of institutional anti-Semitism *without once* bothering to point out that she has yet to produce a single piece of evidence.

What of Berger now? After leaving the Labour Party for the odd, mayfly-like political party 'Change UK' (which seemed to exist purely in the eyes of a favourable centrist media), she subsequently deserted them, when it transpired that no one was interested in their politics, to be an independent MP and then, finally, a Liberal Democrat candidate. On each occasion, the public remained stoically uninterested in the Berger brand of politics. One wonders (though one knows she would never admit it) if she sometimes reminisces regarding those days when she had a committed base of activists, prepared to do the hard work to get her elected, because of their devotion to the party and what they believed it stood for. But perhaps someone like Luciana Berger, a career politician to her core, could never begin to understand such a concept - that of solidarity which, fundamentally, is the bedrock of all socialist parties. One wonders whether she ever reflects that, maybe, she owes those hard-working volunteers an apology. And one also considers whether her complaints of anti-Semitism were ever actually genuine, or were simply attempts to damage a party that she no longer - if she ever had - believed in.

"It is appalling, outrageous and unacceptable that he should be
allowed back into the party."

Margaret Hodge

3 - Chris Williamson - The Making of a Socialist

Like all of those who fell foul of Labour's anti-Semitism battles, Chris
Williamson was a figure of the left. He was not a newcomer to politics
– far from it. One of the increasingly rare cohort of genuinely working-
class Labour politicians (he had worked as a bricklayer and social
worker before becoming a full-time politician), Williamson had been
active in the Labour Party since first joining it, aged 19, in 1976. He
was a politician who, rather than being airlifted into prime seats like the
gilded careerists of the later New Labour years, had grafted his way up
from the bottom, becoming a Labour councillor in Derby in 1991 and
then, eventually, the leader of the Labour council.

Some local antagonists (in the permanently vexed 'Millie Tant' mould)
griped at times about what they considered to be his lack of radicalism
in the early days. And some even saw his later affinity with Corbyn as
opportunistic affectation. For Williamson, though, this would be to
misunderstand his real politics.

Williamson came from humble beginnings. His father was a plasterer,
and his mother a machinist in a textiles factory. He left school aged 15
and worked as an apprentice mechanical engineer for a year, before
leaving to train as a bricklayer. The building industry was notorious for
its poor health and safety record at that time, and this was one of the
grievances that led to the building workers strike in 1972.[67] The
following year, Williamson was working on a big factory extension in
Derby. The health and safety had hardly improved, and he was nearly
killed when he fell 20 feet onto a concrete staircase because no safety
handrails had been fitted to the scaffolding.

When he was 22, he and a friend obtained a market stall in Derby selling wholefoods, but the city wasn't quite ready for the vegan revolution in 1978. The following year, he secured a job under the Labour government's Special Temporary Employment Programme (STEP), with the local social services department, fitting aids and adaptations in the homes of elderly and infirm residents, and disabled people. He eventually trained as a social worker before becoming a welfare rights advocate.

Williamson had been immersed in the labour movement long before being elected to Parliament, and was firmly on the party's left. He was active in his local party from the very beginning of his membership and threw himself into campaigning during and between elections. Williamson served as chair of his local party branch and as secretary of both the Constituency Labour Party and District Labour Party. He was also an active trade unionist, and his fellow workers repeatedly voted him in as their shop steward for the National Union of Public Employees (NUPE) from 1986 onwards, and then as Unison's Amber Valley area secretary ten years later. His trade union activities saw him arrested for obstructing the police when he was picketing his workplace in 1989, during the local government pay dispute, although he won the subsequent court case. Williamson was always prepared to stand up for his principles, whatever the consequences.[68]

Before being elected to Derby City Council to represent the inner-city ward of Normanton, where he was born, he worked closely with Derby's legendary left-wing stalwart David Bookbinder, then leader of Derbyshire County Council. Williamson took on the role of campaign coordinator for the County Labour Party in 1988 when there were moves to ditch Bookbinder following the disastrous city council elections that year, for which right-wingers blamed the county's 'controversial' left-wing leader. The campaign, which Williamson organised, culminated in a landslide Labour victory in the 1989 Derbyshire County Council elections.

As a more senior councillor, serving as chair of housing from 1994, deputy leader for two years from 2000, then as the leader in 2002 and from 2005 to 2008, he implemented a number of innovative measures.

These included assisting people in receipt of social security, developing a long-term environmental strategy to make Derby a sustainable city by 2025, and insourcing as much of the council's work as possible. On the Private Finance Initiative (PFI) issue, which New Labour had substantially expanded, Williamson instantly recognised its numerous flaws. He has been criticised for implementing several PFI projects, as all councils did under New Labour, but he always referred to PFI as "a bullshit scheme". But what was a local authority to do, he asks, when there was no other money available? "We either [do it or] say we are not going to build these schools, or we are not going to refurbish these unfit dwellings".[69] However, he did seek to minimise the negative impact of PFI. For example, he used it to acquire and renovate properties that were unfit for human habitation, so they could subsequently be rented out at low rates to people on the housing waiting list. And he ensured the scheme was modelled to enable the council's building department to bid for the refurbishment work.

Williamson's opponents claim he formed a coalition with the Conservatives when he was council leader in 2006, but that is a caricature of what really happened. It is true that he began a confidence-and-supply arrangement with the Conservatives after Labour lost its overall majority on the council. Securing such an agreement, Williamson maintains, was necessary to avoid losing the council to a Lib-Con coalition. In return for their support, the Conservatives, who were the third-largest group on the council behind the Lib Dems and Labour, were granted three minor portfolios and signed up to nearly all of Labour's programme. It was this arrangement that ensured two further years of Labour governance under Williamson's leadership, enabling: a proactive anti-poverty strategy, including a fair debt scheme and an inward investment strategy linked to decent terms and conditions for workers; a 'neighbourhood agenda' to empower local communities through participatory democracy and devolved council budgets; and a pioneering environmental policy with an ambitious commitment to make Derby a sustainable city by 2025. The reality of this arrangement with Derby's Tories was that Labour called the shots, whilst the Conservative minority was satisfied with a few inconsiderable titles and allowances.

The policies Williamson helped to implement in those two years had a real, material impact on people's living standards and on the city's landscape. For example, the anti-poverty strategy ensured that people who were not claiming their full social security entitlements were actively approached to boost their incomes through comprehensive benefit checks. Meanwhile, the fair debt scheme guaranteed that people who were in debt to the council had their incomes maximised. This more equitable system ensured that any social security entitlements excluded their existing child benefit or disability allowances from their debt repayment arrangements. This meant the repayment regime was considerably lower than that recommended by the Department for Work and Pensions (DWP) for reclaiming overpayments of social security; an act that resulted in the Benefit Fraud Inspectorate threatening to name Williamson in a report as being part of a council that was "too soft"[69] (only to back down when Williamson refused to give any ground).

These progressive initiatives also extended to housing, with the provision of furnished tenancies as well as a moratorium on evictions, except in extreme circumstances, such as heavy-duty antisocial behaviour. As part of Williamson's forward-thinking environmental strategy, the council began building a hydroelectric scheme on the River Derwent. The council's vehicle fleet was also being converted to run on recycled vegetable oil during that time.

Williamson has, in addition, been well ahead of the curve for decades on animal rights and the impact of neoliberalism on farming practices, food futures and disease.[70] He has been a vegan since 1976 and an animal rights activist who has consistently spoken out on these matters.

As a member of the Hunt Saboteurs Association, an organisation in which he played a prominent role in the late 1970s and early 80s, he helped lead the almost 30-year campaign that culminated in the 2004 Hunting Act that made hunting with dogs illegal. Williamson made no secret of his commitment to fighting for animal rights and social justice, and made that central to his campaign the first time he stood for Parliament in 2010.[71]

After he was originally elected as an MP, Williamson used his position to draw attention to these issues and was described as one of the greenest MPs elected in 2010.[72] He denounced the negative impact of fast-food giants. He highlighted how global agribusiness companies are buying up vast tracts of land in developing nations to grow grain for animals, displacing subsistence farmers from their land in the process.[73] And he has consistently spoken out about the impact on public health of the livestock industry, with the Covid-19 crisis being the latest and most deadly example.[74]

Williamson first entered the national scene in 2010 after winning the Derby North seat for Labour with a majority of 613 (the definition of a marginal). It wasn't, however, until 2015 that he came to national prominence as a notable member of the political left, when he and Michael Meacher drafted an open letter to Ed Miliband; a letter, signed by only 16 other Labour MPs, asking Miliband to oppose austerity, bring rail back into public ownership and repeal all the anti-trade union legislation. From that point on, Williamson's profile and reputation amongst the left grew to such a level that, when he lost his seat to the Conservatives by a wafer-thin margin of 41 votes in the 2015 general election, Corbyn would describe his loss as the worst of the night.

Williamson might have got over the line at that election too, but he took a principled stand in opposition to the establishment of a free school in his constituency that an influential group in the local Sikh community were for. It would have been politically expedient to give his tacit support to the idea, but as a conviction politician, Williamson refused to jettison his long-held opposition to free schools in order to curry favour with the proponents of the scheme. In fact, he privately canvassed the Sikh leaders behind the plan to discourage them from pursuing it. Williamson told them that not only did he oppose their idea on political, moral and educational grounds, but it was unconscionable for him to get behind a Sikh free school when he had publicly opposed a Muslim free school in Derby only 18 months earlier.

This principled action on Williamson's part undoubtedly resulted in the loss of this group's support in the general election later that year. The Tory candidate used Williamson's unwillingness to back a Sikh free school in order to ingratiate herself with a community that normally, and overwhelmingly, voted Labour. It saw her, along with prominent Tories from around the country, being invited to speak at Derby's biggest Gurdwara, just before the election, in support of free schools. Previously unheard of, this racial charm offensive led directly to Williamson losing his seat and Derby North becoming England's most marginal constituency. Only Gower in South Wales returned an MP in 2015 with a smaller majority.

In the wake of an electoral defeat like this, parliamentary candidates typically disappear off the scene. For most, there is a shift into a different line of employment. For a gilded famous few, there is the promised land of media work. It is a rare beast, however, who stays on the local scene post-defeat. Very unusually, and as a testament to his devotion to genuine socialism and the Labour Party, this is what Chris Williamson chose to do. Retaining his office in a local shopping centre, Williamson immediately went to work on winning his marginal seat back.

When Jeremy Corbyn secured enough MP nominations to stand as a candidate for leader, Williamson spoke in support of him at numerous constituency party nomination meetings all over the Midlands. The following year he secured a job working as a political adviser to the left-wing Labour MP for Easington, Grahame Morris, just after the attempted PLP coup to force Corbyn out. Although Williamson was working for Grahame Morris, he was formally employed by the Labour Party, which created a problem. Three days after starting his new job, Emilie Oldknow, the then executive director for governance, membership and party services, contacted him to say he needed to amend his social media profiles. She said they created a conflict of interest because they displayed a photograph of Corbyn and Williamson together, and, as a party employee, he could not campaign for a candidate in the 2016 leadership contest. Two days after receiving that message, Williamson tendered his resignation with immediate effect and spent the next two months speaking at local Labour Party nomination meetings as he had done the year before.[75]

In the 2017 general election and following the incredible late surge for the most radical manifesto in a generation, the divide between the PLP and Labour Party *establishment* on the one hand and, the rank-and-file membership and Momentum on the other, was clear. Whilst locally all the funds went to campaigning for Labour legend and veteran MP, Margaret Beckett (of Derby South), it was clear to those involved while campaigning for Williamson's re-election, that something was happening. Volunteers came from far and wide (on one occasion a coachload of supporters from Islington), with scores out campaigning for him on a regular basis. By the eve of the election, it was reasonable to ask if Derby North had ever seen anything like it with hundreds of enthusiastic volunteers combing the streets campaigning for Williamson's re-election.

This grassroots campaign, for someone now very much seen as a figurehead of the left, won Williamson the seat back with a majority more than three times higher than his winning margin in 2010. After being selected as the Labour candidate for Derby North in 2017, Williamson issued a press release stating that he was the most pro-Corbyn candidate standing anywhere in the country, in the most marginal seat in England. It would be hard to see this result as anything other than evidence of the popularity of the more radical version of Labour that Corbyn and Williamson were proposing when allied with a genuine grassroots movement.

After his re-election, there was little chance of Williamson playing it safe. He soon attracted the ire of media commentators and the perennial malcontents of the Labour right in the PLP, who, chastened in the humbling defeat of their chicken coup to remove Corbyn the previous year, were left merely undermining and sniping from the wings. It is, I would contend, impossible to remove the politics from the anti-Semitism wars of these years. Those who wish to keep this issue purely about anti-Semitism either have an ulterior motive for doing so, or are being extremely naïve. Whilst on the surface seemingly unconnected, it was Williamson's involvement with the Campaign for Labour Party Democracy (CLPD) that put him under the glare of the saboteurs' lantern. As these were also, to a man and woman, precisely the same people who were to hound him for 'anti-Semitism', it is worthwhile spending a little time looking at this and considering why this issue caused such grievance on the right.

On the surface, this issue was quite simple. It had been a long-standing aim[76] for activists on the left of the party that Labour MPs, rather than being given a job for life (which it effectively was in many traditionally safe Labour seats), would need to stand for reselection by the local membership. This would, it was argued, shrink the divide between the grassroots membership and the PLP, and make Labour MPs accountable not only for their performance but for their policies too. It would be hard for supporters of democracy to argue against this. As Williamson put it: "I want to see power in the hands of ordinary people. That's what the Labour movement is about".[77] It was hoped that one great consequence of this would be candidates not quite as bereft of local connections and knowledge as, for example, Luciana Berger demonstrated when she admitted her total ignorance of Liverpool legend Bill Shankly.

Whilst seemingly a relatively superficial (yet highly symbolic) matter, this increasing disconnect between Labour and its local working class - the people it was set up to represent - had become something of a crisis. Indeed, it was argued by frustrated activists, that a transition to more local democracy could surely only help. Predictably, however, those Labour MPs less enamoured with democracy - preferring the corridors of Westminster and expense accounts, to actually answering to the people who had gotten them elected - disagreed. For example, ahead of a meeting that Williamson was scheduled to address in Barrow-in-Furness, John Woodcock, the local Labour MP at the time[78], said: "I fear that the prospects of any Labour MP in a seat like mine will not be helped by an appearance from an ardent supporter of the communist *Morning Star* and regular guest on Vladimir Putin's propaganda channel RT. But that is possibly his intention".[79] As always, the real issue of furthering and deepening local democracy was ignored, with the complainant preferring to deal in lazy ad hominem jibes.

It was this active, radical grassroots socialism of Williamson (often on the territory of fellow MPs) which many of Williamson's parliamentary enemies initially objected to. The accusations of anti-Semitism would materialise, somewhat conveniently, later. For stalwarts of the right, Williamson's campaign was an obvious threat to their comfortable livelihoods, and so it is no surprise that many of them were happy to conspire in future attempts to destroy his career.

Allegations of anti-Semitism were, of course, the central issue in Williamson's downfall. But, from the outset, Williamson - unlike nearly everyone else in the party - was not going to express regret for something that he felt was phoney and manufactured.

Williamson signalled his intention to take a different approach in an interview with *The Guardian* on the 28th of August 2017. Readers of this article, coming up against a genuine socialist perspective - a now rare sight in the pages of *The Guardian* - would be left in no doubt where he stood on a range of party issues.

On the wrangling over how the party should pick its next leader,[80] Williamson said: "There shouldn't be a leadership threshold at all [of MPs having to nominate candidates] …. That needs to change. Who are the PLP? They are a tiny percentage of the party. If we're going to have a threshold, it should be CLPs. But that's not the proposition. The proposition is to reduce the threshold. I'll settle for that. Why are people so frightened of democracy?"[81]

These words, simple, straightforward and unafraid, are typical of Chris Williamson. One can immediately understand why they were so thrilling and galvanising for those on the left, wearied by the usual parliamentary standards of double-speak. Williamson was a different and very unusual MP and the threat he posed to the status quo of the Labour Party was obvious; a danger that many in the Labour PLP were not slow to recognise.

When asked a question whether he was concerned over the threat of Labour MPs defecting to other parties due to Labour's new-found radicalism, Williamson was similarly unapologetic: "If people want to go off and stand as independents or centrists around some Tony Blair party, let them go and see how far they get. I don't think it would hurt the Labour Party. If they are neoliberals, they shouldn't be with us".[81]

How refreshing for Labour activists to hear this! Someone finally saying what many felt. Yes, many on the Labour left would echo, if centrist MPs wanted to go to the Change Party (as, in the past, similar types had defected to the Social Democratic Party), the sooner they left, the better.

On the recent Grenfell Tower tragedy where 72 residents lost their lives,[82] Williamson, rather than deal in meaningless mealy-mouthed words of regret and the wish for a future report et cetera, was clear-sighted in what he saw as the failings: "It's important we do find out how and why it started but there are deeper questions that relate to the political culture that allowed it to happen. It's a culture that has afflicted both Labour and Conservative governments, starting with Margaret Thatcher. That whole culture is built on deregulation, privatisation and cuts".[83]

Politicians, Williamson continued, who had "foisted neoliberal brutality on this country" had contributed "directly to Grenfell Tower and these people have blood on their hands who have pushed this approach".[83] Oof! Rarely, in modern times, has a British politician spoken so starkly and clearly about a different approach to society; socialism in other words.

Inevitably, the issue of anti-Semitism was discussed. Williamson gave such allegations a straight bat, saying rows over Corbyn's handling of anti-Semitism within Labour and his approach to Venezuela were "proxy wars and bullshit". "I'm not saying it never ever happens but it is a really dirty, lowdown trick, particularly the anti-Semitism smears. Many people in the Jewish community are appalled by what they see as the weaponisation of anti-Semitism for political ends".[83]

How different this combative, dismissive rebuttal - of what Williamson rightly understood to be politically motivated smears – was to the normal mea culpa and crocodile tears, which were quickly becoming de rigueur. How refreshing, for once, to hear someone's genuine opinion and not have to wade through, as Williamson put it, "bullshit".[83]

It was during this time - able as he was to galvanise and energise the left with his eloquent exposition of a socialist vision for the party - that Williamson's stock rose. He was in demand to speak at members' meetings up and down the country, and by media outlets as a very rare example of a socialist MP; a token defender of this scarcely heard viewpoint. Consequently, it was during this time, that he became a marked man by the PLP - someone who posed a threat to their cosy Westminster club and their comfortable lives.

A short time after the interview with *The Guardian*, on the 2nd September 2017, Williamson joined a 'picnic for Palestine' event in his constituency – a small, local gathering by a pro-Palestinian rights group. Afterwards, he shared a tweet that incorrectly attributed an anti-Israel quote to Nelson Mandela. The quote, superimposed on top of a picture of Mandela, read: "Israel. It has systematically incarcerated and tortured thousands of Palestinians contrary to the rule of international law".[84] The outcry that followed was predictable.

The *Jewish Chronicle* deemed this 'incident' worthy of a full article, leading with: "Williamson is embroiled in further controversy after sharing on social media a notorious faked Nelson Mandela quote that compared Israel to apartheid-era South Africa".[84] Of course, the fact that, while admittedly false, it was not anti-Semitic, was not commented on. Nor, explicitly, the fact that it wasn't created by Williamson (Users of social media are aware of how easy it is to share false content mistakenly.) And, when informed it was inaccurate, Williamson promptly took it down.

Despite the reasonableness of all this, those who wished to be mowed down by an invisible car duly lay in the road and played the victim. Ironically, the words themselves, sentiments which Williamson and many on the left would wholeheartedly support, were ignored. And for anyone familiar with Nelson Mandela, it would seem that, while he didn't express himself this way, he would likely have lent his full support; just as, earlier in his life, he commented on the similarities between the African National Congress (ANC) and the Palestinian Liberation Organization (PLO): "We identify with the PLO because just like ourselves they are fighting for the right of self-determination". Moreover, the following quote, from that same Mandela speech in 1997, is widely known: "We know too well that our freedom is incomplete without the freedom of the Palestinians".[85]

In addition, I find the ensuing quote even more relevant to the position Labour supporters of Palestine find themselves in today: "The temptation in our situation is to speak in muffled tones about an issue such as the right of the people of Palestine to a state of their own. We can easily be enticed to read reconciliation and fairness as meaning parity between justice and injustice. Having achieved our own freedom, we can fall into the trap of washing our hands of difficulties that others face". One can imagine that if Nelson Mandela were active in today's Labour Party, he would quickly be silenced and accused of anti-Semitism, just as Williamson and others have, for refusing to "speak in muffled tones".[86]

Aware of what was occurring - the growing clamour for vengeance from his political enemies, articulating itself under the cover of 'anti-Semitism'- Williamson was, understandably, keen to get on the front foot, to refute certain accusations. In September 2017, he gave two interviews, one to *Tribune* magazine and one to talkRADIO, where he attempted to put the record straight. Predictably, the mainstream coverage of these interviews was shallow and misleading, so they deserve some attention here.

In the pages of *Tribune*, a long-standing Labour-supporting magazine, Williamson outlined his surprise "that I was the target for much of this twaddle. The old 'reds under the bed' guff was dusted off for another outing, malicious accusations of sexism and anti-Semitism were thrown around like confetti".[87]

On the resistance of the PLP to the campaign for more internal democracy, Williamson had this to say: "Much to the chagrin of media commentators and *New Labour* throwbacks, some constituencies have had the temerity to elect officers who reflect the views of party members. This seems to have come as a shock to those who prefer backroom deals, but members actually prefer open democracy to stitch-ups".[87]

He added: "The accusations of anti-Semitism were positively sinister and followed my lengthy interview with *The Guardian* newspaper in August. In it I said that many people in the Jewish community had told me they were appalled by what they had publicly described as the 'weaponisation of anti-Semitism'. I also stated that false allegations were a 'dirty, lowdown trick'. This led to demands for me to be sacked from the frontbench because, it was claimed, I was denying anti-Semitism existed, which I wasn't. Some even made the highly offensive and hurtful suggestion that I was an anti-Semite myself, yet I have fought racism all my adult life, from the 1970s when I was active in the Anti-Nazi League".[87]

Whenever this straightforward argument is made - 'I won't be apologising for anti-Semitism, because I think these allegations are false' - it seems entirely reasonable and inarguable. None of us, for example, would expect to have to keep apologising for littering the street when we know that we are not the ones responsible. It is the strange triumph of the witch-hunt to make such common sense logic somehow incredibly controversial and beyond the pale.

In his interview with talkRADIO on the 20th September 2017, Williamson said the following: "I know some people have expressed anxiety, and the abuse online is unacceptable, but that isn't from Labour Party members. There's no evidence as far as I'm aware [that] any of the abuse online is being perpetrated by them. The party National Executive Committee agreed tough new rules on racism, anti-Semitism, or any forms of bigotry, because hostility and prejudice have no place in the Labour Party. Indeed, if there is evidence it came from party members, they have no place in the Labour Party. Clearly, we want all communities, faiths, people of no faith, to feel comfortable inside the party".[88]

Again, one might think, on the surface, these comments were uncontroversial and beyond debate. Williamson repeats the Labour Party's commitment to fighting racism in all its forms, including anti-Semitism. He also states that he has yet to see any evidence of anti-Semitism from Labour Party members. It remains baffling, therefore, how these simple statements and honestly held opinions became so explosive.

It was during this time that the Campaign Against Antisemitism (CAA) was prevalent in the news. Its opinions, keenly sought by media organisations, were nearly always received with meek and unquestioning acceptance; the modern Labour Party and the media's simple reasoning being that if the CAA proscribes something as anti-Semitic then it, de facto, is.[89]

Should the neutral observer take the CAA advice seriously? In its grandly titled 'Antisemitic barometer' - given considerable, unquestioning attention when released - we see this entry for 2018: "The leader of the once fiercely anti-racist Labour Party is now the candidate of choice for anti-Jewish racists". And this, for 2020: "Our already-anxious community has been subjected to a harrowing ordeal by Mr Corbyn and his allies".[90] How should one react to such ungrounded, misleading hyperbole? One could, of course, compare these incendiary accusations to the reality i.e. Corbyn's record on these issues in Appendix III. One could, alternatively, ignore them as the vexed ravings of unsound minds. Unfortunately, the Labour Party and the mainstream media chose neither of these approaches, preferring instead to receive such 'pronouncements' as matters of grave fact which needed acting upon urgently. It would be laughable if it weren't so tragic.[91]

As well as defending himself, it should be noted, Chris Williamson wasn't going to let others be falsely accused. Nor would he ever meekly walk on by. Speaking, in May 2018, at a rally in Manchester in support of Labour activist Marc Wadsworth, expelled for anti-Semitism, Williamson stated, "Many people in the Jewish community…said to me that anti-Semitism was being weaponised. I think some people have weaponised it".[89]

It was this steadfast refusal to give any credence to the witch-hunt that so enraged his enemies; Margaret Hodge being at the top of that list. In July 2018, seemingly in a state of unbridled fury due to the Labour Party not summarily adopting the IHRA's working definition of anti-Semitism wholesale, she confronted the leader of her own party, in the Houses of Parliament, and called him a "fucking anti-Semite and a racist". She went on: "You have proved you don't want people like me in the party". And how did Corbyn respond to these ludicrous comments? By asking her if she needed a sit down and a cup of tea? By calling for assistance in recognition of her tempestuous state? No. "I'm sorry you feel like that,"[92] were his words. True to form, no matter how base the insult, Corbyn never responded in kind.

Somewhat incredibly, Hodge had now learned "what it felt like to be a Jew in Germany in the 30s". In an interview with Sky, she recalled what her "dad used to say……. He always said to me as a child: 'You've got to keep a packed suitcase at the door Margaret, in case you have ever got to leave in a hurry'".[93]

That an MP should make this direct link between Corbyn, the Labour left, and the Nazis, is repugnant. And it is ironic that, while member after member in the Labour Party has been suspended for 'bringing the party into disrepute', the self-styled 'Hero of Barking' is allowed to continually voice her shameful opinions and is actually feted for them.[94]

If the party at large, and the entire political commentariat, were not going to object to these comments in the slightest way, then Williamson would not be so reticent. In an interview with Sky News, he said: "I think she's indulging in a degree of hyperbole there to say the least. The reaction that I've seen from the wider general public is that they are bemused - some are pretty angry actually that she sought to make such a comparison. It really does trivialise the terrible horrors of the

Holocaust and to somehow try to create some equivalence with that horror with receiving a letter from the general secretary of the Labour Party is pretty abhorrent".[95]

It would be comments like these that earned Williamson the undying wrath of the 'anti-Semitism' lobby. It was this defence, and the defence of others on the left, that, rather than be taken at face value simply stoked in his enemies reticence and subversion, thus labelling him a 'Jew baiter'. And, tragically, such methods worked.

Over the months that followed, Williamson would not hold back his opinions when asked for them. On the 23rd September 2018, as a guest speaker at a Labour Against the Witch-hunt meeting, he compared the 'witch-hunt' (against members accused of anti-Semitism) to George Orwell's *1984*, where "good is bad, black is white and we had the Ministry of Truth and all the rest of it".[96]

Echoes of the censorship in Orwell's dystopian vision were evident the month after this speech, when the Sheffield Labour Students club cancelled an invitation for him to speak after complaints from the Sheffield Jewish Society alleging that Williamson's actions had encouraged "a culture of anti-Semitism".[97] One looks, as usual, quite fruitlessly for any shred of evidence in relation to these accusations. Arguably though, despite these continual skirmishes, the three *major* incidents that were to decide Williamson's future in the party were to come, one after the other, from the end of 2018 into 2019. We shall look at each in turn.

GILAD ATZMON

If an individual could summarise the complexities inherent to this sorry tale, then Gilad Atzmon's tangled backstory gives the lie to the often oversimplified way this whole narrative is presented in the media.[98]

One thing that strikes the casual observer straight away is that Atzmon - a character so openly called out as an anti-Semite - is Jewish.[99] Born in Tel Aviv, he grew up in Jerusalem, served in the Israeli Defence Force (IDF) and took part in the 1981 war against Lebanon. All these things, one might have thought, would surely mark Atzmon as someone untouchable by the Zionist lobby. It is a common observation, though, that no one earns more vitriol than someone perceived by a community to be a deserter, a traitor.

Atzmon pulled no punches in his political views. He was, he stated, "a Jew who hates Judaism", "a Hebrew-speaking Palestinian", someone who had realised that "his people were living on stolen land". And he went further. Not to be scared off by those who believed such opinions were taboo, Atzmon openly compared Israel's policy to that of the Nazis, describing the treatment of the Palestinians as "genocide".[100]

All of these views, while hotly disputed both inside Israel and out, are - or at least should be - legitimate ones. For, if one believes that it is an apt comparison to make (the treatment of Palestinians in the occupied territories by Israel and the treatment of Jews by the Nazis), then why can't one make it?

One should accept that, on a handful of occasions, Atzmon probably expressed views that one could interpret as anti-Semitic. In 2003 he wrote a blog article critical of Zionism: "[We] must begin to take the accusation that the Jewish people are trying to control the world very seriously".[101] One could argue that this is merely clumsy writing, and the fact that he subsequently altered 'Jewish people' to 'Zionists' shows that Atzmon agrees. And perhaps he overreached in his statement. Rather than trying to control the world, perhaps Atzmon meant that the Zionists were exerting their substantial influence in order to control any debate around Israel; a nation very much at the heart of world geopolitics. Still, one must accept that welding Jewish people to a worldwide conspiracy should be given short shrift.

Whether this makes him an 'anti-Semite' is another matter though. Especially if given the time and space to defend, and expand on, such views (which Atzmon usually did in a way that would make such convenient categorisations more difficult). And if this incident (and a handful of others, over many years, whilst operating in a highly fraught and vexed political arena[102]) still leads one to adopt a position of censorship then that is, of course, an entirely different thing. The question of no-platforming is a complicated one, with passionate adherents on both sides.

It was into these fraught waters that Williamson was to sail, somewhat unwittingly, in December 2018. As a celebrated saxophonist, Atzmon was due to play with the band, the Blockheads, in Islington. Islington council, after the predictable uproar (that if they let Atzmon play they would be culpable in their "support"[103] of anti-Semites) quickly moved to cancel the performance. On the morning of 21st December 2018, Williamson retweeted, without comment, a petition against this ban.

The response wasn't long in coming. Jennifer Gerber, director of Labour Friends of Israel (LFI), told Politics Home: "Sadly this is the latest in a long line of despicable actions and comments by Chris Williamson. Unfortunately, an apology alone cannot and will not absolve him from the hurt he has repeatedly caused to the Jewish community." And, from the same article, Ivor Caplin, chair of the Jewish Labour Movement (JLM), tells us that "Gilad Atzmon is an anti-Semite. Chris Williamson is a Jew baiter".[103]

When one speaks to Chris Williamson, however, his version of the event seems very relatable. He was, he says, travelling back from London when he got a text from a friend. His friend was upset, Williamson relates, that the Blockheads were prevented from performing at an Islington venue on the grounds that one person, the text read, had complained to the council; the gist of this, that if Atzmon were present, it would make him/her feel 'uncomfortable'. Williamson, at that point, had no idea who Atzmon was, but his friend described him as a Jewish Israeli IDF veteran. That knowledge, combined with Williamson's own recent experience, appeared to him at the time another plausible example of the ongoing witch-hunt. His friend asked him to share the petition, which he did (although he never signed it).

Lee Garratt | 57

Within ten minutes, Williamson had received a call from Asa Winstanley, associate editor of Electronic Intifada, suggesting that he might want to take it down as there will be "a load of shit coming your way".[69] Williamson promptly did, but Michael Segalov, *The Guardian* journalist and 'paid-up' member of the witch-hunt (always alert to heresy), had already taken a screenshot and was now demanding an apology. The inevitable escalation and furore that ensued followed the predictable playbook.[104] It was seemingly ignored that Williamson had, by now, deleted the original tweet and, in two follow up tweets, messaged: "I've learned that Atzmon, a former Israeli soldier, is not confined to the jazz world. I am told that in various blogs and in speeches he has adopted anti-Semitic language. I wasn't aware of this until after I tweeted the petition".105

As always, there seems to be a range of banal, calculated responses to Williamson's actions. None of them, though, could legitimately or seriously claim that his actions were "despicable" and those of a "Jew baiter"; the difference between action and offence unfailingly vast, yet treated as Siamese-like.[103]

MOMENTUM MEETING

We have already seen, with his involvement in the CLPD, Williamson's commitment to grassroots action. It was a philosophical approach that separated and distinguished him from many of his peers in the parliamentary party who, on ascending to Westminster, increasingly saw their role defined by the Machiavellian power struggles within its corridors. Williamson came from a different tradition where power ultimately came from the rank and file.

It was in this tradition that, on Saturday 23rd February 2019, Williamson attended a meeting at the behest of Sheffield's Momentum branch. As he recalls, the meeting went well, with an enthusiastic and friendly audience who responded favourably to his calls for greater democracy within the party and gave their full-blooded support for a more radical socialism.

The gathering was videoed and shared on social media by the Momentum branch as they felt it had been a hugely successful and highly motivational meeting. But a political correspondent for the *Yorkshire Post* who saw the video on the internet shared a selective extract of the footage. In the days to come, it was this excerpt from Williamson's speech - presented without any context - that was to cause uproar.

Williamson had told the meeting: "The party that has done more to stand up to racism is now being demonised as a racist, bigoted party. I have got to say I think our party's response has been partly responsible for that, because in my opinion...we have backed off too much, we have given too much ground, we have been too apologetic".[106]

One might see this as merely a comment on the party's strategy. Others viewed it differently, however. Luciana Berger, now departed from Labour, declared: "This is what I have left behind. It's toxic. Our country deserves so much better".[106] *The Guardian* columnist, Jonathan Freedland, went further. He wrote: "Labour's insistence that the party is an implacable foe of anti-Jewish racism is rendered laughable every day that Chris Williamson remains a Labour MP".[107]

The same day as Freedland's article was published, Wednesday 27th February 2019, Williamson got a call from Amy Jackson, then the PLP liaison officer in the leader's office. "Chris, get in the office, you're fucking leading every news story", he recalls her saying. On his arrival, he found the atmosphere frenetic. They were, Williamson states, "running around like headless chickens". Jeremy Corbyn was due at Prime Minister's Questions (PMQ), and there was a distinct nervousness that the latest anti-Semitic brouhaha around Williamson would wrong-foot him. Williamson recalls Seumas Milne, Corbyn's chief aide, stating: "Well, look, if there is going to be an investigation [into Williamson's comments] Jeremy should announce that at PMQs". At this point, Karie Murphy, the chief of staff, "exploded" in Williamson's words, saying that Jeremy didn't want any investigation.[69]

As a favour to Jeremy Corbyn and the LOTO (Leader of the Opposition) staff, Williamson prepared a statement offering a qualified apology saying he was sorry if his words had caused offence. He was told that this would draw a line under the matter. Predictably, Theresa May used the opportunity to exploit the issue during PMQs in response to Tory MP, James Cleverly.[108] Williamson wasn't in the Commons chamber and watched the proceedings on TV in the leader's office. However, before he left, the Labour Party's general secretary, Jennie Formby - a putative Corbyn supporter - telephoned Karie Murphy to say she was mounting a formal investigation after all, even though Williamson had been assured less than an hour before that by issuing a statement it would be the end of the matter.

The statement read: "I deeply regret, and apologise for, my recent choice of words when speaking about how the Labour party has responded to the ongoing fight against antisemitism inside our party. I was trying to stress how much the party has done to tackle anti-Semitism".[109] Williamson now regrets issuing the apology, but says it was done in the heat of the moment.

As Williamson notes, the Labour Party's default position - when exposed to furious but unsurprising allegations from critics - was never to challenge, no matter how dishonest or fraudulent, and *always* concede; the exact, woeful strategy he had decried at the Momentum meeting days earlier.

He left the parliamentary estate and went to the nearby Red Lion pub, a favoured haunt of politicians. He met with a friend there and discussed how they should respond to the forthcoming investigation. Williamson remembers that, at some point, he received a call from Karie Murphy on his mobile and went outside to take it. In the conversation that followed, he was informed that his situation had been elevated from an investigation into a full suspension. While he was still speaking to Murphy, he saw a Sky TV camera crew approaching, who proceeded to film the remainder of his telephone conversation. That this wasn't a coincidence was clear from their first question to him: "What's your reaction to being suspended?"[69] One wishes one were surprised that someone from within the leadership team could think it fitting and appropriate to tip off the media before informing Williamson. Naïve and trusting folk might think there is an innocent explanation for this. But this leak follows a consistent pattern of undermining and impeding by the Labour Party, where other high-profile victims of the witch-hunt similarly discovered that the media had been briefed beforehand.

Soon after this statement was released, in a planned move, a spokesman for Jeremy Corbyn announced that Williamson had actually been issued with a "notice of investigation" but would remain a Labour member while a "pattern of behaviour" was examined.[110] If this, and Williamson's apology, were meant to defuse matters, then they demonstrably failed. Tom Watson, the ever-dependable deputy leader, speedily rowed in, stating "It is not good enough. If it was in my gift, I would have removed the whip from him already".[109] He wasn't alone. A letter, signed by 38 Labour MPs who were members of the Tribune group, was delivered to Corbyn's office reiterating that Williamson "should have his membership suspended."[111] In a very unusual step, former leader Ed Miliband rang Corbyn and said that if Williamson was not suspended by the end of the day, thirty MPs would be leaving the party.

Rarely, if ever - in modern British political history - have so many felt entitled to use a single issue like this as effective blackmail. Whether Williamson's apology would have been enough to fend off critics for another day must remain a moot point, for, on the same day that the Tribune group of MPs delivered their letter, news broke of another incident.

WITCHHUNT FILM SHOWING

Unfortunately, Williamson wasn't alone in being the victim of spurious and politically motivated attacks, under the cover of 'anti-Semitism', in the party. Across the country, Labour members, in varying positions of power, were being dragged into the wider investigation of what, by now, had become a witch-hunt. One of the more prominent victims was Jackie Walker, a black Jewish woman who was an influential figure and activist on the left, and had once risen to become vice-chair of Momentum. A documentary film, aptly titled 'WitchHunt', was made with her as the central figure, which examined the anti-Semitism wars in the Labour Party and highlighted the attacks on anti-Zionist Jews inside the party.[112]

It is a film of vital importance to anyone interested in this whole, disheartening affair. A sober and nuanced reflection on the role that weaponised claims of 'anti-Semitism' have played in the party, it includes contributions from many well-known figures in the movement. And it has received many plaudits, including words from Mike Leigh, internationally renowned film director: "This impeccably executed film exposes with chilling accuracy the terrifying threat that now confronts democracy, and the depressing intractability of the Israel-Palestine situation".[112]

Williamson was approached in February 2019 by the Jewish Voice for Labour group (JVL) about whether he could book a parliamentary committee room for a showing of the film. The JVL had formed in 2017, frustrated at what they saw as the dominant BoD narrative in the Labour Party and society at large. This narrative, indicating that Britain's Jewish community was under siege and facing an existential threat by an anti-Semitic left, was rejected outright by JVL as false and driven by an unrepresentative, political sect (namely the BoD and newspapers such as the *Jewish Chronicle*). Furthermore, they dismissed it as patronising at best that a single, official viewpoint should be attributed to a group as diverse as Britain's Jewry.

Williamson agreed that by organising a public showing of the film - a film of obvious contemporary importance - within the Houses of Parliament, this would be a valuable addition to an important debate. For, he reasoned, if such matters are not open to discussion within these ancient debating walls, then where could they be? (This held particular resonance as a planned screening of the film at the Labour Party conference a few months earlier had to be cancelled when the venue received a bomb threat for agreeing to host it.[113])

One might have thought that the showing of such a thoughtful and intelligent film, considering the ongoing issue at the heart of the party, would have been welcomed. Labour MPs such as Ruth Smeeth, however, were cheerlessly and depressingly not interested: "Giving these people and Jackie Walker a platform at the home of British democracy is a complete and utter disgrace," she blustered. A Labour 'spokesman' said it "was completely inappropriate"[114] for Williamson to have booked a room for its showing. One could strenuously ask 'Why?' to both utterances and hope that the platitudes subside. The Labour Party, however, had now evidently taken an official position that it was not suitable or proper to even *discuss* the very thing which weakened it.

The usual pressure was brought to bear on Williamson, and the meeting was eventually cancelled at his behest. Williamson relays how he was in the process of giving a tour to the Jewish members of the JVL - the group who had initiated the film screening - when he received a message from Jennie Formby demanding that he cancel the showing, with a heavy hint that if he didn't, she would suspend him. The Labour Party was, once more, adopting the bizarre position of caving in to fears about being labelled anti-Semitic by cancelling a meeting that was actually wanted and desired by a Jewish organisation.

Again, one is left baffled how a Labour MP could be condemned for merely wanting to show a film which stimulated discussion on a topic of vital importance to the party. It seemed that the Labour PLP preferred to mimic the actions of the fabled ostrich when confronted with a problem.

Pathetically, by the evening of Wednesday 27th February 2019, the Labour Party caved in again, suspending Williamson from the party. This, despite him acquiescing to the demands to cancel the meeting. Throughout this whole process, it is notable how promises - both verbal and formal - have been broken by the Labour Party in their dealings with Williamson, who has consistently tried to act in good faith.

It is worth highlighting an excerpt from *The Guardian* at that time, which stated: "The Guardian understands that there was also considerable disquiet among Labour staff about the decision not to suspend Williamson while his case was considered. "'After a coordinated push we got them into the right place,' said one senior party source".[109] The actions of this avowed, anti-Corbyn clique, right at the heart of the party, came to light over the following months.

Asked now about this issue, Williamson has only one regret. And it is a bitter one. The apology he felt pressured to give was not genuine. He felt then, as he feels now, that there was simply nothing to apologise for. And he remains, to this day, perfectly happy with his choice of words at the Momentum meeting. That he produced the apology under duress, and with an understanding that the issue wouldn't be taken any further, gives Williamson little solace. It merely proves the point he was making at the meeting: that apologies, as well as being unnecessary, are monumentally stupid strategically and merely give credence to the initial complaint. If they are intended to dissuade and defuse those attacking you, they fail, time after time after time, and simply embolden bad-faith actors to go further; seeing climb downs, appeasements and capitulations as targetable stress points and weakness.

Shortly before his suspension, Williamson recalls a meeting he had with Jennie Formby, then General Secretary of the party. She told him she gets more complaints about him than every other member of the party put together; to which Williamson bluntly stated "If that's true it's just proof of a concerted smear campaign".[69]

There seems to be a tendency throughout this crisis to conflate a mass of allegations as meeting the burden of proof, rather than an examination of the 'evidence' itself. For whilst it appears to some 'common sense' that there can be 'no smoke without fire', one also sees just how easily situations can be abused. Jonathan Freedland, for example, in his later articles, simply refers to a long list of alleged crimes - each one easily refutable.[115] However, by now, such inconvenient rebuttals did not matter; allegations themselves were all-powerful and omnipotent.

Williamson relates, at this point in the proceedings, Formby did seem to agree that - for the most part - the complaints against him were nonsense. However, when he responded that she needed only to tell them to "fuck the fuck off", she became "irritated".[69] At that point, the meeting descended into ill-temperedness, with Formby moving on to Williamson's democracy roadshows.

He recalls Formby stating: "If I was an MP, I'd be pissed off if you came into my constituency". And: "You're not Jeremy, you know".[69] This criticism implied that Williamson was being too 'busy' and a troublemaker and therefore struck him as peculiar. For wasn't this his job? And he saw anti-Semitism - real or fabricated - as an incredibly important issue. As he recollects, *all* of the democracy roadshow meetings were extremely positive. For they had arisen from the defeat on this issue at the Labour Party conference. And, for those of a similar mind to Williamson, they were very inspiring to see (internal party democracy a live issue worth fighting for).

Williamson remembers trying to explain this to Formby and Karie Murphy, who was also present, but described both of them as not being interested. A short time later, Williamson says he received the bad-tempered email from Formby implying he would be suspended if he didn't cancel the 'WitchHunt' film showing. Williamson complied (another decision taken under duress which, today, rankles). Typically, later that evening, despite the assurances he felt he had received regarding his apology and despite the agreement he had regarding cancelling the film, Williamson was suspended anyway.

When Williamson, a short time later, received the formal letter of suspension from Jennie Formby, it included a fateful paragraph:

"The pattern of [Williamson's] behaviour has included allegations of campaigning in favour of members who have been formally disciplined by the Party for antisemitism; failing to delete retweeted material from a holocaust denier, even after it was pointed out to you that the retweeted account belonged to an individual with such unacceptable views; tweeting and signing petitions in support of an individual who a Labour council had refused to allow to perform in their premises because of the individual's history of antisemitism; sharing platforms and giving public praise to people with a history of allegations of antisemitism against them; publicly attacking the BoD, just hours after a synagogue suffered a mass shooting in the United States, which caused deep fear among every [sic] Jewish household. A range of other allegations have also been made against you, but the list above is sufficient for the time being to indicate the pattern of behaviour to which I refer".[116]

'Pattern of behaviour' became a phrase the Labour Party repeatedly used in its suspensions; an easy way of merely listing a whole range of allegations without ever having to establish if any of them had any credence. Williamson's blatantly unfair suspension was not without opposition. True to the phenomenon in the recent annals of the Labour left, this was *not* led by the Socialist Campaign Group of Labour MPs, but by the wider base. Many CLPs rallied to Williamson's defence, passing motions of support. These varied slightly from branch to branch, but a flavour of their overall sentiment can be seen in the wording of the Sheffield Hallam CLP (which passed by 40 votes to one) whose motion said: "The allegation that Chris is downplaying antisemitism is totally unfounded. His comments, made at a Momentum meeting in Sheffield, were taken out of context in a deliberate attempt to ruin both the reputation of Chris Williamson MP and Jeremy Corbyn".[117]

Labour HQ, perhaps spooked by this intemperate show of support from an unruly base (not so happy to go along with these blatant injustices as the Socialist Campaign Group seemingly were), issued orders from the top. In a dress rehearsal of what subsequently happened in the aftermath of Jeremy Corbyn's suspension, word came down that CLPs were not to accept such motions as they were prejudicing the disciplinary procedure and therefore could not be taken into account.

One can sympathise with this to some extent, but also question its relevance. The membership naturally wanted to affect the disciplinary procedure, but many of them simply did not want Williamson subjected to it in the first place. And as for the NEC not taking such motions into account, one wonders how many motions are earnestly considered by them anyway. Submissions of this kind are the standard working practice of the Labour Party's internal democracy, yet a mere whiff of censure from the top is enough to cow the more passive CLPs and those who just want to get by without stirring up perceived trouble.

Shamefully, one such example was Williamson's own constituency of Derby North which, inexplicably, maintained a vow of silence throughout the crisis (something that persists to this day). As a local Williamson supporter, I attempted to move one such motion of support at the CLP meeting, only to be told that such things had to come from the electoral ward. At the next electoral ward meeting, I was duly informed that motions were the business of the CLP, not that of the ward (accompanied by mutterings of the branch being closed down)!

It was through similar, nakedly opportunistic deploying of bureaucratic red tape that democratic debate was stifled up and down the country. Fortunately, this reticence in addressing difficult things - preferring to stick to safe, parish-pump issues such as bin collections and litter - wasn't universal. Despite the disapproval of the Labour Party, over 30 CLPs and a variety of trade unions and other organisations passed motions of support.

As is usual with complaints of this kind, the party machinery did not move quickly. However, after four months of deliberation[118], Willamson's suspension was finally lifted, and he was reinstated. In a statement, the party announced that: "A party panel, advised by an independent barrister, had found Williamson breached party rules and issued a formal sanction, though chose not to refer him to Labour's highest disciplinary body, the National Constitutional Committee, which considers possible expulsions".[119]

One might consider such a decision - given the circumstances - faintly ludicrous or very harsh, but to the right wing in the PLP, and its fellow travellers in the media and elsewhere, this was nothing short of a disgrace. The reactions it evoked, to give the reader an idea of the strength and scale of the continued assault against Labour members who dared transgress from what was becoming the official party line, were many.

Ruth Smeeth called Williamson's re-admission "disgusting" and said she was "horrified." What was lacking, of course, was any kind of exploration by the oddly incurious press. What was it *specifically* that she was horrified by? Fellow MP Jess Phillips also claimed to be "disgusted", suggesting that Williamson should have been expelled.[119] The chair of the Jewish Labour Movement (JLM), an avowed Zionist organisation ostensibly of 'Labour supporting members of the Jewish community'[120], said: "How dare the Labour Party deny it is institutionally racist against Jews when it decides to take no action against Chris Williamson".[119] No one, it seemed, within the party, aside from Williamson himself, was prepared to call out this whole charade for what it was.

One thing that is clear from dialogue with Williamson is just how aggrieved he feels at the almost total lack of support received from fellow MPs, particularly the Socialist Campaign Group of Labour MPs (being one of its most outspoken and active members). He recalls a conversation with Laura Pidcock on the day he was suspended. She was secretary of the Socialist Campaign Group and, whilst upset at what had happened, told Williamson that he should not attend any SCG meetings while he was suspended.

There were a few exceptions to this lack of solidarity. Williamson recollects how the MP for Crewe and Nantwich, Laura Smith, was very supportive and repeatedly, but ultimately unsuccessfully, attempted to persuade the Socialist Campaign Group to issue a collective statement of solidarity with Williamson. He also remembers Fabian Hamilton, the Jewish MP for Leeds North East offering his backing privately. Williamson says Keith Vaz too, was at times supportive, telling him verbally in passing - in the division lobby - that it had been "crazy" and "absurd" what had happened to him and that he had written to Formby to express this opinion.[69] Indeed, as Vaz himself (not known for being a firebrand of the left) pointed out, from a politically expedient angle, the best chance Labour had of winning Williamson's marginal parliamentary seat was for him to remain as candidate.

Predictably, in the face of overwhelming pressure from Labour MPs and accompanying howls of outrage from the corporate media, the Labour Party, in a similar fashion to how it had acted at *every stage* of this process, once again relented. Only the flimsiest of reasons was given for this democratic outrage. Keith Vaz, who had been on the panel that decided to re-admit Williamson, suddenly said that he felt he had been put in that position at the "last minute" (even though he was taking medication because he had been unwell) so the decision should be "reconsidered".[121] It duly was and, within 48 hours, Williamson was re-suspended.

So many questions arise from this. How much pressure was exerted on Vaz which prompted this frankly embarrassing last-minute revelation? If what Vaz said was true, why hadn't he aired his concerns earlier? And why, indeed, didn't anyone else question his involvement? The courts did not take a kindly view of this farce in the months that followed. In Williamson's view, Formby very likely panicked. And pressure was undoubtedly applied to Keith Vaz, in something of a pickle of his own, resulting in his capitulation (with who knows what agreement or deal in place).[122]

"Someone must have slandered Josef K., for one morning, without having done anything truly wrong, he was arrested."
The Trial, Franz Kafka

4 - High Court - Justice Served?

It is important to remember that, focused as we are on the travails of the Labour Party, the events in this book were taking place against the backdrop of a national crisis - Brexit. And, with this all-consuming story in the headlines day after day, it became increasingly apparent that Prime Minister Boris Johnson would take a calculated gamble and call for an early election in the hope of securing an increased majority.

Given this, and the urgent imperative for incumbent Labour MPs to do well - especially in knife-edge marginals such as Chris Williamson's Derby North - you would be forgiven for thinking that the Labour Party might have felt the need to accelerate matters; especially given that Williamson had been suspended for months prior to his initial reinstatement!

Unfortunately, the Labour Party didn't see things this way. And, as the weeks and months dragged by with no sign of a final decision, they were clearly comfortable, for reasons unknown, for this whole sorry affair to be prolonged. Williamson thus felt he had no option but to take legal action in the High Court.

In view of the likelihood of an early election, Williamson's lawyers applied for an expedited hearing, but this move was resisted by Jennie Formby. This refusal to speed the process up resulted in three preliminary hearings where the Labour Party's lawyers argued that there was no evidence of an early election being called. They said Williamson was merely "speculating" about such a possibility and cited the Fixed-term Parliaments Act 2011 as justification for their submission.[69] Each time, however, the judge rejected the party's representations and, finally, at the third hearing, the judge dismissed Labour's concerns and set a date for the full hearing to take place.

Within 36 hours of that decision, and just six days prior to the listed High Court hearing, Williamson received a letter from the party's Governance and Legal Unit. They claimed fresh allegations had been made against him, so they were imposing another suspension! The letter stated:

"We note that you are currently suspended pending the determination of charges of alleged misconduct against you by the National Constitutional Committee. We write to give you formal notice that it has been determined that the powers given to the NEC…should be invoked…in relation to the new allegations…to suspend you from office or representation of the Party, pending the outcome of an internal Party investigation. Please note this administrative suspension shall continue until the Party has concluded this new investigation and determined its outcome, irrespective of what may be determined in relation to any previous allegations of misconduct for which you are suspended."[123]

So, in plain speak, in a twist familiar to readers of dystopian novels such as *Darkness at Noon* (relating the nightmarish qualities of Soviet bureaucracy), Williamson was being informed that, regardless of how the current court situation resolved itself, he would still be suspended. Williamson's legal team felt that this was a clear attempt by the party to subvert a court ruling that was likely to go against it. Williamson, therefore, asked his lawyers to request that the judge consider making a ruling on this last-minute ruse by party bureaucrats to abuse the process.

The letter went on to say: "It is important that these allegations are investigated and the NEC will be asked to authorise a full report to be drawn up with recommendations for disciplinary action if appropriate."[123]

One can speculate on the procrastination by the Labour Party in two ways. The first is that the party was acting in genuine good faith. And, in its noble pursuit of the 'truth', it was prepared to jettison any hope of an electoral victory in order to give Williamson and the Labour Party, as a whole, the time required for a full and thorough investigation.

The second, slightly more earthly possibility, is that in letting the months slide by interminably with no resolution, the party hacks' continued inability, or rather *unwillingness*, to come to any decision over a relatively straightforward matter, allowed them to get rid of a troublesome MP by default. As Williamson was technically suspended, he would be unable to contest his seat, necessitating a stand-in. It goes without saying that, if this analysis is correct, then such politics or actions belie the honour and decency meant to be at the heart of the Labour Party.

A lingering question remains: Why, when it was self-evidently so damaging to the party, was there such reluctance from Labour to deal with this issue? The longer Williamson's case was in the public eye, the more disruption it caused. Why would any political party therefore wish this upon itself? There are two reasonable answers. One, like a boy reluctant to remove a splinter from his thumb, there was notable disinclination within the party when facing up to the painful reality. Labour's position had become one of pusillanimous retreat when faced with pressure, accompanied by very little moral volition.

The other is a more malevolent reading. That there existed individuals who knew that this situation was damaging to elements within the party they disapproved of (specifically those, like Williamson, perceived to be on the Corbyn wing) and so delighted in any obfuscation and delay. Such a reading shifted from the left fringe, widely derided as crank and conspiratorial, to the mainstream in the wake of the explosive, leaked report - a story which I will come to later.

Whatever the truth, what is undeniable is that the financial burden to the party, and its members, was huge. Chris Williamson's legal fees alone were £89,000. And he estimates the total legal fees to be around

£200,000 as Formby had instructed a QC to represent the party. One doubts very much that many members would consider this an effective use of their hard-earned money.

The new allegations levelled against Williamson were, if anything, even more risible and unimaginative than the first set. One was from an offended Conservative voter who had sent an abusive email to Williamson referring to his criticisms of Margaret Hodge for drawing an equivalence between the persecution of the Jews in Nazi Germany, and her receiving of a letter from the Labour Party stating she might face possible disciplinary action.[124]

This Tory supporter objected to Williamson's response, referring her to a video that had been recorded by the acclaimed Jewish academic, Professor Norman Finkelstein. In the video, Finkelstein lays out, in stark terms, his disgust at Hodge who compared her experience of receiving a disciplinary letter with the experience of her parents who lived through the Holocaust. As part of his unsparing commentary, Finkelstein said that Hodge was: "cheapen[ing] and exploit[ing] the memory of Jewish suffering"; "trivialising the memory of the Holocaust"; and he requested that she "get the hell out of the Labour Party".[125]

Tragically, in the brave new world of the Labour Party, a single complaint against a Labour MP (sharing the honestly held views of a celebrated Jewish professor) was deemed to merit investigation and ongoing suspension. Why these comments were seen as unduly "offensive" and "personal", yet Hodge was given vituperative free rein with no consequence remains something of a mystery.[123]

Another preposterous allegation against Williamson related to his response when asked by journalists about complaints from certain Labour MPs, like Ruth Smeeth and Wes Streeting, regarding him speaking at various fringe meetings during the 2019 Labour Party conference.

Streeting said: "It beggars belief that people are still willing to give Chris Williamson a platform given his conduct. As he is suspended from the Labour Party he should not be speaking at events at our conference". Smeeth also waded in, adding: "This is inappropriate on every level and the Labour Party must make sure it does not indulge this kind of activity. He is currently subject to a disciplinary hearing – on that basis, he should not be granted a pass to conference and nor should he be turning up to wind everyone up."[126]

You can kick a man while he's down, but retorts are evidently not permitted. Williamson responded by saying:

"It's a tragedy that a tiny but noisy minority of party members want to trash the spirit of the Human Rights Act. It's one of Labour's greatest achievements. Maybe these malcontents have forgotten that Labour enshrined freedom of expression into British law nearly 21 years ago. If these mischief-makers are genuinely interested in winning the next election, they should pipe down and devote their energies to exposing the Tories and promoting a common-sense socialist programme. That's the way to beat Boris Johnson, rather than attempting to censor the voices of people like me, who speak for the overwhelming bulk of party members and the vast majority of Labour supporters."[127]

But Williamson's defence of his right to free speech, and his call to arms that all party members should be focused on promoting Labour's message and exposing the Tory government, didn't impress Labour's Governance and Legal Unit. In a letter to him, they asked why he had made the comments in the first place and thoroughly scrutinised his words: "Who did you intend the terms 'malcontents' and 'mischief-makers' to refer to? " and "Please explain what you meant by 'they should pipe down'?" (see Appendix VII). The depths to which the party's functionaries and bureaucrats sunk were quite extraordinary and eerily forbidding.

The justification for the original suspension included an article that Williamson had shared on Twitter from the left-wing media site Skwawkbox, which referred to the president of the BoD being accused of sharing an antisemitic trope.[128] In his accompanying tweet,

Williamson made the ironic remark, "blow me down with a feather".[129] Unbeknown to Williamson, tragically, on the same day (27th October 2018), a lone gunman had opened fire in a Pittsburgh synagogue, leaving 11 people dead and six others injured.[130]

It is hard to follow the logic or veracity of the witch-hunt argument at times; people *choosing* - quite cynically and disingenuously - to link entirely unconnected events for political capital. An anti-Semitic attack - no matter where in the world – which coincides with remarks able to be exploited, will always bring about disapprobation, but we must remind ourselves: some people will stomp up and down whatever the weather. Tweets meeting the Labour Party's new standards of propriety presumably now have to include saccharine tears and outpourings of faux grief. But the fact that Williamson was both unaware and satirical was conveniently used by his adversaries to claim he was revelling in his imputed role as "Jew-baiter".[107]

Williamson makes it abundantly clear that he did not know about the incident in Pittsburgh on the day he shared the tweet, having been occupied at a conference. This was met with incredulity by some, but rings true for many who first heard about the Pittsburgh incident through the response to Williamson's tweet.[131]

Back on safer ground, following an all-day High Court hearing on 12th September 2019, Mr Justice Pepperall reserved his judgment, which he eventually delivered on the morning of 10th October 2019. It was an outright victory over the decision to reimpose the suspension two days after it had been lifted. The judge determined that:

a) The Labour Party had failed to follow the rules in this case saying "*the evidence indicates that in practice the rules are not strictly followed*";

b) The Labour Party's evidence on the health of Keith Vaz MP (which did not even include a statement from Mr Vaz or other panel members) was "*unsatisfactory*" and that "*it would be surprising if, as an experienced Parliamentarian, Mr Vaz: (a) had taken part in an important meeting if he felt himself unfit to do so; and (b) then failed clearly to make that point in his subsequent email [to Ms Formby]* ";

c) "*breach of confidence was not of itself a proper reason for reopening the decision*;" and

d) if the Labour Party wanted to argue that reopening the decision could have been justified because it was "*mired by political interference, or the appearance of political interference*", as advanced for the first time at the hearing, then "*it should have filed evidence dealing with the point.*"

Consequently, the court concluded that "*it is not...difficult to infer that the true reason for the decision in this case was that members were influenced by the ferocity of the outcry following the June decision.*"[132]

Moreover, contrary to the submissions of the Labour Party that it was appropriate to take account of such an outcry in a disciplinary matter, the court found that:

"*The NEC should decide cases fairly and impartially in accordance with the rules and evidence; and not be influenced by how its decisions are seen by others. Internal and press reaction to a decision is not of themselves proper grounds for reopening a case that was not otherwise procedurally unfair or obviously wrong.*"[132]

In short, then, and to summarise, the court found that Chris Williamson had been treated unfairly and unlawfully by the Labour Party in re-suspending him after an NEC panel reinstated him. In terms of the additional suspension that was imposed the week before the hearing, Judge Pepperall said: "*While the Labour Party is no longer able lawfully to pursue the original disciplinary case against Mr Williamson, that does not afford him immunity from any subsequent disciplinary action... [the court] should not micro-manage the [party's] disciplinary process...[so] the new disciplinary case must run its course.*"[132]

In light of the court's leniency on the final point it was not a total victory for Williamson, but certainly a one-sided judgment with a little Clay-Liston ointment and the Labour right as the big, ugly bear. Finally, therefore, one hoped that legal clarity might be able to cut through the obfuscation and misreporting, both from the Labour Party and the media. Incredibly, this was not how the corporate media hacks described the outcome.

The Guardian led with the headline "Chris Williamson loses legal bid over Labour Party suspension".[133] ITV News covered it with "MP Chris Williamson loses High Court battle to be reinstated to Labour Party".[134] The BBC declared "MP Chris Williamson loses anti-Semitism appeal".[135]

So, what had happened? Had we finally fallen down the rabbit hole and ended up in a legal wonderland where up was down and vice versa?

Insanely, in terms of the court case itself, this entirely misleading coverage rests on the relatively minor fact that the judge had decided that the most recent suspension must be allowed to run its course. One might disagree with the judge's findings on this particular point. It might strike one as wrong and a blatant abuse of the system for the accusing party to keep a process alive by simply 'finding' new accusations (as if their level of gravity is worthy of the name), thus continuing to kick any sense of justice further down the road. And, one might ask, doesn't a process such as this ultimately hand power in these legal games to the accuser? Even allowing for this, to describe the judge's decision to tolerate the most recent disciplinary case as a victory for the party seems bizarre.

Examining the mainstream media's coverage of the case however, one struggles to find any prominence given to the main finding, that the Labour Party's re-suspension of Williamson was unlawful. Indeed, so one-sided is the general reporting of the story that when Williamson states that the court ruling was a "clear victory for justice and due process", that it was a "damning indictment of our party's internal disciplinary procedures" and that the party's bureaucracy "had been defeated in the courts" it seems, in this context, like a non sequitur.[135]

The way the legal costs were allocated gives the lie to the Labour Party's claims of a legal victory. The Labour Party had been demanding that Williamson should pay up to 60% of their legal costs (even though they had lost the main argument). The judge's view on this depicts things in a rather different light compared to the skewed impression one might have drawn from the media coverage at the time: awarding Williamson the entirety of his costs incurred up to 3rd September 2019.[136] It is neglectful and astonishing that the corporate media's reporting of this case remains so wildly inaccurate and unbalanced. Whilst it is undoubtedly pertinent that Williamson remained suspended, one would have hoped that the media outlets had a greater allegiance to the facts and findings than their toil suggests.

This reveals another frustration. Time and again, it has been shown that such dubious charges and allegations can, after much effort and expense, be successfully rebutted in the courts. However, as in this case, there is very rarely any significant coverage of these successful challenges, and it is left to the committed few to scan the small print for any mention. So, there was no mainstream media coverage of Williamson's victory on this point. The Labour Party did not have to provide an apology in the face of media criticism because there simply wasn't any of real note. One does not have to be on the left to find something chilling in the media's ability to manufacture a convenient 'truth'. It was around this time that many of us realised the true importance of what Winston had meant in George Orwell's seminal text, *1984* (Nineteen Eighty-Four), when he, speculating on the nature of truth, said: "Freedom is the freedom to say that two plus two make four. If that is granted, all else follows."[137]

It is a bitter irony then, that despite this huge, largely successful legal fight, despite the enormous amount of energy and money expended, at the end of the court case, Williamson - because of the fresh raft of insincere and bad faith allegations - remained suspended. And, predictably, despite Labour's legal team claiming that there was "no evidence"[69] of an early election, less than three weeks after Judge Pepperall delivered his verdict, a general election was called.

Interestingly, around this time, Williamson, by chance, met Corbyn in the Parliament corridor behind the speaker's chair. (Williamson and Corbyn remained on friendly speaking terms whenever they met.) Corbyn told Williamson that he had "spoken to the NEC", that it would be "all sorted", and that he would be the "Derby North candidate" in the upcoming election. Williamson also had a few phone calls from Seumas Milne during this period, trying to persuade him to make a further statement of contrition. Williamson recalls a particularly ill-tempered conversation where Milne, much to Williamson's annoyance, kept asserting that there was a "real issue with anti-Semitism in the party". And so, Labour Party logic goes, one should keep apologising.[69]

Williamson refused to make any further statements, however. And he now sees these qualified apologies as a trap. As has already been noted, Williamson regrets his apology over the Sheffield Momentum meeting. This was made at the behest of the party alongside an assurance that the matter would not be escalated, but, as we know, following a pattern of duplicity the Labour Party adopted from the outset, it *was* escalated. Furthermore, Williamson's 'apology' was used as ammunition by the witch-hunters as proof that he had done something wrong; that he was, in fact, guilty of an anti-Semitic act, when in reality nothing could be further from the truth.

After months of 'bad faith' treatment by the party, Williamson's position hardened. He now told the party that if he wasn't going to be reinstated, then he would be standing in the forthcoming election as an independent candidate. Furthermore, if the Labour Party was genuine about retaining the seat, he remained the only serious choice. But this was about more than personal pride and success for Williamson. As someone whose reputation had been dragged through the mud, he felt there ought to be some sort of admission or recognition that the party's petty bureaucrats can't keep treating people like this in a carte blanche manner; that someone had to take a stand in order to demonstrate that there should be consequences for their faceless, "unfair, undemocratic and authoritarian behaviour".[69]

One would have hoped, during these long, arduous and lonely battles against the might of the Labour establishment and their many influential supporters in society at large, that Williamson would have had at least *some* support from his fellow 'socialist' MPs. There had been precious little of that up to this point. Indeed, it was only after he had been initially reinstated that Williamson directly asked for a public expression of support from his fellow Labour MPs in the Socialist Campaign Group. He requested a collective statement of solidarity as a response to the motion, signed by around 150 Labour MPs and peers, calling for the whip to be withdrawn from him for a year.

Williamson remembers Richard Burgon saying, in answer to his request, "What can 10 MPs do against 100?"[69] No collective statement was ever given - no solidarity ever offered. As any activist on the left knows, what ultimately lies behind any manifesto promise or economic policy is something essential and eternal. Solidarity. The age-old commitment that, however few in numbers one might be, one does not cross the road when one sees someone in need. It is safe to say that the Socialist Campaign Group's actions during this time were symptomatic of the PLP as a whole and will not be entering the hallowed halls of left solidarity and fighting spirit.

Oh, and what did Williamson do with the monies from the legal settlement, the reader might be wondering? Use them to go on a well-earned holiday? Pay off his mortgage? No, true to form for this lifelong socialist, he ploughed the money into a fighting fund[138] for others on the left. So if those perhaps less fortunate than him ended up in the British justice system fighting similar allegations (but without the money to contest them) they now had a lifeline. One wonders how many of Williamson's critics would have done a similar thing?

> "'It is not necessary to accept everything as true,
> one must only accept it as necessary.'
>
> 'A melancholy conclusion,' said K.
> 'It turns lying into a universal principle.'"
>
> *The Trial,* Franz Kafka

5 - Starmer, Panorama and the Leaked Report

If Labour members - many of whom were simply tired of this endless anti-Semitic 'crisis' - hoped that the election of Keir Starmer as leader would, if not bring the crisis to a close, then at least take it off the front pages, they were to be sadly mistaken.

They might, quite reasonably, have had optimism for this. Following the disastrous election defeat of December 2019, held in the toxic shadow of Brexit, Jeremy Corbyn - for so long the totemic figure of the left - resigned. With his departure, and others on the left taking more of a back seat (and Chris Williamson, as we have seen, being forced to resign), one might have sensibly expected the oxygen to be taken from the anti-Semitism debate, fixated, as it always had been, on the left. Perhaps, many hoped, the whole issue might now become - as it arguably should have been in the first place - a niche, internecine issue. Unfortunately, for all concerned, we didn't have to wait long for the issue to raise its ineradicable head again.

The first resurgence of the anti-Semitism war came by surprise and, in many ways, was self-inflicted. Starmer, elected in April 2020 as Labour's more centrist numero uno, had always talked tough on anti-Semitism as part of his leadership pitch. He wanted to "tear out [the] poison by its roots", he had asserted time and again on the campaign trail.[139] This worried many on the left, fearful that such talk was yet another example of the Labour Party kowtowing and giving credence to lies; an act of self-harm that, if emanating from an individual, would require intervention in the form of therapy and counselling.

Even some of Starmer's ardent supporters were stupefied by his actions in the aftermath of what seemed, at first, to be a very minor social media 'incident'. On the 25th June 2020, *The Independent* published a lengthy article on the famous actress Maxine Peake, well known for her outspokenness in defence of Corbyn and left politics in general. It was a wide-ranging article which touched on Peake's upbringing, her support of Labour and Corbyn, and her most recent film work. On the day the newspaper was published, the Shadow Education Secretary Rebecca Long-Bailey (or RLB as she is commonly referred to) shared a link to the article on her Twitter feed.[140] This wouldn't have startled any of her followers, given that it was an article championing Labour by a long-standing and well-known supporter who was, actually, one of RLB's constituents. So far, so normal.

Unfortunately for RLB, however, it wasn't long before the social media witchfinder generals had fixed on the following quote, attributed to Peake, in the article: "Systemic racism is a global issue....the tactics used by the police in America, kneeling on George Floyd's neck, that was learnt from seminars with Israeli secret services."[141] This was, it was argued, Peake indulging in an apparent anti-Semitic theory whereby, once again, the Jews were being held responsible - on a global scale - for pernicious things. And, their logic went, RLB, in retweeting this article, was intensifying the deep-rooted anti-Semitism of the Labour left.

Even by the very low standards of the ongoing witch-hunt, this seemed like an odd argument on many levels. For example, if you actually read the article, one sees (immediately following the contentious quote) the following disclaimer from *The Independent*, "('A spokesperson for the Israeli police has denied this, stating that "there is no tactic or protocol that calls to put pressure on the neck or airway"'.)"[141] Still, after a few frenzied hours where Labour HQ demanded withdrawals and apologies from RLB (arguably the only prominent member of the left remaining in Starmer's shadow cabinet), she was summarily sacked from the front bench.

A series of tweets followed from RLB, which seemed eminently reasonable. The "main thrust of the article", she rightly pointed out, was criticism of the Conservatives and, ironically it turned out, calls for "Labour unity". RLB also points out what should be blindingly obvious to anyone, anywhere, who decides to share an article: "In no way was my retweet an intention to endorse every part of that article."[142]

Even for some of Starmer's more vehement supporters, his actions seemed at best odd and at worst a misguided and needless opening of old wounds. Of course, some of the hysteria generated by this article can be explained by the context of the times. Black Lives Matter had exploded onto the scene after the video of George Floyd being subjected to a neck restraint (dying at the hands of US police) had gone viral.

The logical leap required in alleging that Israeli security forces were implicated in the Minneapolis Police Department's training (which resulted in the neck restraint) marked a new low for the witch-hunters. For suddenly, it seemed, an additional example of anti-Semitism had been found. (One is reminded of Clover and Benjamin discovering that the commandments had been changed in *Animal Farm*.) Once upon a time, to be an anti-Semite, you had to be involved in saying or doing pronounced anti-Semitic things, but that had now changed. To the people after the scalp of RLB (and Peake), it was now possible to be an anti-Semite simply by inferring that Israelis were connected to bad things, in whatever context; even an event as seemingly uncontroversial as claiming Israeli involvement in US police training.

Now, whether this is right or wrong[143], one notes that at no time does Peake ever use the word 'Jew'. She merely refers to the state of Israel. So, bizarrely, we were in the position of those seeking outrage simultaneously taking the next step – conflating Israel with the worldwide Jewry; the very thing that was seen as an example of anti-Semitism in the IHRA code that these same people had been desperate to adopt. (One could say that we now had people using anti-Semitism to claim anti-Semitism.)

Starmer and his inner circle had no doubt though: "The article Rebecca shared earlier today contained an antisemitic conspiracy theory."[144] One notes the use of the past tense, for this was now, in the Labour Party of 2020, an established fact. When it came to all things Israel, one could no longer simply be 'wrong' or 'factually incorrect'. No. Any implied criticism, even if inferred, was high-rise anti-Semitism and reported as such. What was noticeable, through its customary absence, was any serious questioning by the mainstream media regarding the validity of this approach.

One can only conclude that this was politics as optics. Forget the outdated concept of the 'truth'- this was about how things are *perceived*, one can imagine Starmer's inner circle arguing. For, you can picture his advisors neatly suggesting, that by sacking RLB, Starmer was demonstrating to the media that here was a new leader showing a decisive break with dodgy, anti-Semitic Corbyn.

Things settled down in the wake of this for a few weeks. With hindsight, it seems to have been the quiet before the storm. And when the storm finally broke, it was over an issue that the Labour Party had been quietly trying to fudge and kick down the road for the last twelve months.

In July 2019, an episode of the BBC's flagship current affairs programme, Panorama, was broadcast, entitled 'Is Labour Anti-Semitic?'[145] The programme made for a very frustrating hour and largely consisted of vague allegations from Labour staffers which, when looked at for more than a few seconds, didn't stand up to any serious scrutiny. Many, indeed, stretched credibility to breaking point. For example, one witness claimed, as a Jewish Labour member, that she was regularly exposed to comments such as "Hitler was right".[145] For anyone involved in the Labour Party at any level, it is difficult to tally or correlate such outright hate-speak with the reality experienced. And one wonders why, if this was the case or argument being presented, that further details weren't forthcoming. Who was the person behind such an outrageous statement? Where were they based? Were they reported to the police? John Ware took the default media position of accepting the allegations at face value, rather than believing they merited any further investigation; the predictable next step, in this now well-trodden form of journalism, castigating Labour and Corbyn for their lack of action.

Indeed, for many observant viewers, the lie regarding the fundamental issue was actually hidden, in plain sight, in the programme itself. Asked by Seumas Milne how Labour should deal with the 'crisis', Mike Creighton, Labour's director of complaints at the time, stated that Corbyn should give a speech "saying that Israel had a right to exist".[146] So, as much as Jonathan Freedland and Tom Watson pontificated that this wasn't about stymying criticism of Israel, when it came down to it, the whole anti-Semitic issue could be seen as a political row by invested lobby groups over the status of Israel.

And the nature of the complainants on the programme was never clearly established for the audience. Viewers were not told, for example, about the background of the young woman who, at the start of the show, tearfully declared that the Labour Party was no longer a "safe place"[145] for Jews. Onlookers might have felt it quite beneficial to be informed that this was Ella Rose, who had left her job at the Israeli embassy to take up a position with the Jewish Labour Movement. They might have preferred to be informed that the same Ella Rose, along with other officials from the Jewish Labour Movement and elsewhere, had been exposed in an undercover operation by Al Jazeera as colluding with Shai Masot; Masot, an Israeli embassy official (who was hurriedly removed following the screening of the damning documentary), attempting to discredit British politicians who were seen as a threat to Israel. In Ella Rose's case, she can be seen on camera threatening Jackie Walker, the Jewish Labour activist, with physical violence, bragging she could "take her out" with her Krav Maga skills.[147] It is staggering that Panorama thought it appropriate to use such a compromised character as their opening witness in the programme.

Professor Alan Johnson was another given the opportunity to express his view that "You can say the occupation is wrong, you can say the settlements are wrong", but what you cannot do is call Israel an "inherently racist endeavour".[145] One notes, again, that Panorama failed to inform the viewer that Johnson was in the pay of the 'British Israel Communications and Research Centre', one of Israel's main lobby groups in the UK. (However, at least by laying out the issue in such politically stark terms, the programme performs the service of allowing the frustrated viewer to see what truly lay behind so much of this.)

One would think that even the most casual student of modern history would see, given the primary role that Zionists have played in creating the modern state of Israel, that referring to it as a racist endeavour is a legitimate opinion. Not least because there is a clear hierarchy of treatment in relation to each race. (Veterans of the struggle against apartheid in South Africa, including Archbishop Desmond Tutu, say the treatment of the Palestinians by the Israeli regime is worse than the apartheid they experienced.[148]) One might disagree with this observation. One might think it overly simplistic. But surely any reasonable person would consider it a point of view worth debating and not dismissing as the Labour Party had done with its usual anti-Semitic steer. And if Labour really did want to choose such a path, then it should recognise that it has taken the same line of argument as Israel itself and all its lobby groups.

Time and again, in this whole sorry saga, viewers/readers are not given the necessary full context to make an informed view. The Panorama programme is symptomatic of this. Former Labour MP Louise Ellman,[149] for example, is given ample opportunity by the programme to claim that hard-line Corbyn anti-Semites had aggressively taken over her Liverpool constituency.[145] Not once did the show allow an opinion from any of her numerous local critics, some of them Jewish, who claim that none of her complaints were genuine. Moreover, there is the assertion that her stance was readily inspired by her political antipathy towards an internationalist, anti-imperialist socialist left. And that it was *her* who had been guilty of spreading false information and orchestrating a bullying campaign against local socialist members. Thanks to the Jewish Voice for Labour (JVL), though, there exists a thorough, exhaustive account of what happened in Liverpool Riverside over the years in question, none of which was ever referred to in the Panorama programme.[150]

As has been said, most of the witnesses in the programme were taken from one group, the Jewish Labour Movement (JLM). And many of them also came from Labour's disciplinary unit. Some of these names were to become much more familiar to Labour supporters over the months that followed the show's transmission. At that time, though, these witnesses, as befitted their position as mostly young, inexperienced members of Labour's Governance and Legal Unit, were not widely known. Following the broadcasting of the programme in July 2019, in a rare moment of fight, the Labour Party issued a complaint which, amongst other things, noted, "the tendentious and politically slanted script; the bias in the selection of interviewees; and the failure to identify the political affiliations or records of interviewees in a highly controversial, sensitive and contested subject produced a programme that was a one-sided authored polemic".[151]

Following this, seven of the Labour staffers and John Ware himself (named as "unsuitable"[152] in Labour's complaint for previous form and hostility towards Corbyn) launched legal action against the party for defamation. A year later, despite widespread belief in the party that they had a solid legal case, Keir Starmer caved in. An apology (where have we heard that before) was read out at court for "defamatory and false allegations" made by the party to the complainants, and then, to add insult to injury, the complainants were paid out an estimated £500,000 in damages.[153]

Members up and down the country were incensed at this craven surrender. They were even more angered by the sums involved; their membership fees, in effect, greasing the palms of, or enriching, the enemy within. Renowned film director, Ken Loach, was particularly eloquent in his criticism: "Keir Starmer will have used his much-praised 'forensic' skills to examine these accusations in great detail. Can party members, whose funds will be used for the pay-outs, see his rigorous interrogation of the evidence, including the leaked emails, that led to his apology in court? We would hate to think Starmer has sacrificed principle for a quiet life."[153] Ouch!

At this point, any party members who had laboured in the belief that the anti-Semitism witch-hunts would, with the accession to power of Starmer, be quietly drawing to a close, had a rude awakening. For Starmer, it seemed, was bent on pursuing this issue as doggedly as the most fervent Zionist, no matter what the cost to the party. And what made this decision all the more galling to Labour members was that they now knew more about the complainants' nature and political disposition - some of which was quite shocking.

In April 2020, an internal report by the Labour Party examining the handling of the anti-Semitic complaints was leaked to the media (who the guilty party was remains a mystery). This report resulted from an internal investigation into the party's Governance and Legal Unit and was intended as a submission to the forthcoming EHRC report. What it contained, it is fair to say, was explosive.

Even for hardened political observers, the quantity and nature of the politically motivated abuse aimed at the Corbyn operation, quoted from emails and social media messaging services, was truly noxious. Corbyn's first wife had left him, one member of staff declared, "because he was such a boring Trot".[154] A misogynistic streak was very evident in relation to Corbyn's chief of staff Karie Murphy and political secretary Katy Clark – both victims of insults and slurs, including "fuckwit"[154], "Medusa", "pube head", and "smelly cow".[155] Unsurprisingly, many of those involved were the same people subsumed in the witch-hunt.

Sam Matthews, for example, was another young member of Labour's Governance and Legal Unit (GLU), heavily relied upon in the Panorama hit job. Looking shaken, viewers had heard him claim: "For the first time it became immediately apparent to me that there was a really, really extensive problem with anti-Semitism at that stage. For the first time that I had noticed, people who held deeply anti-Semitic views were feeling like the Labour Party was their home."[145]

Readers of the leaked report, however, soon discover that he was part of a right-wing faction that "openly worked against the aims and objectives of the leadership"[154] - running a project in the 2016 leadership election to suspend Corbyn supporters ("a trot hunt"[156]) and, in the 2017 general election, secretly diverting funds from key marginals towards right-wing factional allies. And, we learn, he was only given the job in the first place courtesy of a nod and a wink from friends in the right places who happened to share similar political views.

Dan Hogan was another influential witness, again from the GLU, used by Panorama. We hear him voice, with pseudo exasperation: "Is 15 people expelled satisfactory enough for a crisis that has been running three years?"[145] The same Dan Hogan, it transpired to readers of the leaked report, told a fellow staff member that someone who whooped during a Corbyn speech, days after his victory, "should be shot"[156] and that "Jez's speech was a total crock of shit".[154]

These offensive comments were in keeping with Hogan's political views however as, in 2015, he had made a sarcastic reference to Labour's policy on having an EU referendum as making "a change from Trident, rail renationalisation and landlord-bashing". He also seemed in shock at John McDonnell's tax policy, stating to a friend: "Brace yourself. McDonnell just called for corporation tax to go up," which garnered the response, "You're kidding me".[154]

Time and again, in the leaked report, one sees the visceral hate that members of Labour's inner sanctum had for their own left-wing members, expressed here by Hogan bumptiously asking, in September 2015, "Is Labour in the South East just full of Trots?"[154]

Of course, Hogan's political views do not stop him from having genuine, well-founded and reasonable arguments about anti-Semitism. Repeatedly though, one saw that those making the complaints were, almost without exception, on the right of the party and, to add insult to injury, had form when it came to criticising the left. So when evidence came to light of them being in an organised cabal, using their position to undermine and discredit the left by whatever means necessary, it caused many to question the sincerity of their anti-Semitism complaints. Indeed, it was these same people who had worked tirelessly to undermine their own democratically elected leadership, rather than tackling genuine anti-Semitism (The Labour Party, against good legal advice, rolling over and using members' hard-earned subscriptions to pay off these erstwhile party staffers.)

Over the next few weeks, the divisions in the party were laid bare. In perhaps the most significant move, Len McCluskey, general secretary of the powerful Unite union, expressed anger at his members' money being used in this way, calling it a "clear miscalculation" and a "quite extraordinary" decision.[157] And this was no mere front, or token show of anger for the cameras. A few weeks later, in a move of utmost seriousness for the Labour Party, the Unite union announced that it was cutting its affiliation money to the party by about 10%. The 'anti-Semitism crisis' was now affecting the Labour Party in real cash and political terms.

It has been typical of the anti-Semitism 'crisis' of the last few years that, just as one episode started to die down (it is telling that none of these separate issues ever entirely went away as none were adequately resolved), another one arose to keep the story on the front pages. And, arguably, this time, it would be the biggest story yet.

"'If there's no meaning in it,' said the King,
'that saves a world of trouble, you know,
as we needn't try to find any.'"
Alice in Wonderland, Lewis Carroll

6 - The EHRC Report

On the 29th October 2020, the Equality and Human Rights Commission (EHRC) finally released its long-awaited investigation report. This report had commenced the previous May, after complaints to its body by the Campaign Against Antisemitism (CAA) and the Jewish Labour Movement (JLM), who both claimed that Labour was not compliant with the equalities law. When the EHRC announced its intention, such news was hugely significant - the body had previously investigated only one other political party, the openly fascist British National Party (BNP). Gideon Falter, the chief executive of the so-called 'Campaign Against Antisemitism', could not conceal his delight. He said, in a tone more suitable to a movie trailer: "In just four chilling years", the Labour Party had "become a home for hatred in British politics".[158]

Given its scope, given the considerable coverage it had and continues to receive - in view of the response generated from within the party - one could arguably see the EHRC report as the apotheosis of the whole 'crisis'. In its pages, one finds a summary of the main complaints. In its analysis of the issues, one detects - sometimes by omission - a valuable precis of the main protagonists' arguments. And in its reception, one sees the fault lines and implications for the party moving forward, possibly for years to come.

The key findings of the EHRC could be summarised as:

- the leadership could have tackled anti-Semitism more effectively "if the leadership had chosen to do so". Note that no individuals are ever named who should have "tackled anti-Semitism more effectively".[159]
- "there was political interference in the handling of antisemitism complaints", stating that this was "indirectly

discriminatory and unlawful" (one of the examples given was the handling of a complaint regarding Corbyn and the mural in London's Hanbury Street, by the Los Angeles-based street artist Mear One).[159]

- that the Labour Party breached the Equality Act in two cases where two individuals were found to be engaged in "committing unlawful harassment", including using "antisemitic tropes and suggesting that complaints of antisemitism were fake or smears".[159]

- Ken Livingstone was one of these two named cases. The specific instance it referred to was his defence of Labour MP, Naz Shah, who had shared on Facebook an image - that had initially been posted by Jewish academic, Professor Norman Finkelstein - of Israel on a map of the USA with the words "problem solved". "Ken Livingstone repeatedly denied that these posts were antisemitic," the EHRC said. "In his denial, Ken Livingstone alleged that scrutiny of Naz Shah's conduct was part of a smear campaign by 'the Israel lobby' to stigmatise critics of Israel as anti-Semitic, and was intended to undermine and disrupt the leadership of Jeremy Corbyn MP". In conclusion, the EHRC said Shah's comments "went beyond legitimate criticism of the Israeli government" and were not protected by rights to free expression. "Neither is Ken Livingstone's support for those comments," the EHRC added.[160]

Pam Bromley was the only other named individual, a Labour councillor in Rossendale, Lancashire. On 15 December 2019, she put a post on Facebook concerning Jeremy Corbyn: "My major criticism of him – his failure to repel the fake accusations of antisemitism in the LP [Labour party] – may not be repeated as the accusations may probably now magically disappear, now capitalism has got what it wanted." This, the EHRC concluded in its wisdom, consisted of "unwanted conduct related to Jewish ethnicity" and "had the effect of harassing Labour Party members".[161]

That such a seemingly comprehensive report of the 'crisis' ultimately resulted in just two people connected to the Labour Party being mentioned directly, namely Ken Livingstone and Pam Bromley, is somewhat surprising. The truth is that the EHRC was originally planning to name *six* individuals in order to justify its conclusions against the Labour Party. One of those was Chris Williamson, who they had initially accused of acting unlawfully and harassing the Jewish community, but his name was removed from the final revised report after a swift and comprehensive legal challenge; a move testament to the absence of any credible evidence against him and one which, furthermore, made his suspension from the Labour Party all the more egregious.

Regarding Livingstone and Bromley, the allegations the EHRC list as proof of anti-Semitism collapse under the slightest investigation. Livingstone is implicated on the strength of him not recognising Shah's comments as being anti-Semitic. Which, of course, they are not. Whilst someone might reasonably disagree with, or take offence at, Shah endorsing the satirical relocation of Israel to the USA, anti-Semitic it certainly isn't.

Likewise, the evidence given as proof of Bromley's anti-Semitism is, if anything, even weaker. All Bromley had done was state that she believed accusations of anti-Semitism inside the party were fake. One is reminded of the famous medieval trial for witches: if they drowned, they were innocent; if they lived, they were guilty and would be burned at the stake.

That such a weighty and influential report could, after all this time, only find two instances of 'anti-Semitism' which, upon investigation, proved to be groundless, is astonishing. What also beggars belief is that nowhere, throughout its entire 130 pages, is there any definition of what anti-Semitism actually is. Conveniently, the vagueness that subsequently follows from this failure to define what is being talked about, allows the EHRC to ramble on at length regarding what it sees as Labour's failings on this issue.

Also, the fact that this very high profile report was initially launched using complaints from flawed bodies such as the JLM and the CAA, should give any neutral observer pause for thought. And that it delivered its findings on such an 'existential' threat of 'institutional' anti-Semitism from a paltry 70 complaints over a three year period, leaves one with the perception that it had very little to go on.

The Labour Party, of course, did not react with the scepticism this impaired report deserved. Keir Starmer chose to see its publication as marking a "day of shame" for the party. He felt, despite a lack of evidence within the report, that another apology was warranted. "We have failed Jewish people, our members, our supporters and the British public," he said. "And so, on behalf of the Labour Party: I am truly sorry for all the pain and grief that has been caused."[162]

Sadiq Khan, influential London Labour mayor, likewise saw it as a "dark day" and "utterly shameful" that the Labour Party had overseen "unlawful acts of harassment and discrimination".[163] Presumably, Khan is referring to Livingstone and Bromley where, on both counts, there is a total lack of either.

The witchfinder generals were, of course, jubilant. Chief among them was Margaret Hodge, who crowed bitterly, obsessed as usual with evil Corbyn, "It happened on his watch. He shamed the Labour Party. He sat at the centre of a party that enabled anti-Semitism to spread from the fringes to the mainstream." She added: "He is yesterday's man. He is absolutely irrelevant."[163]

Berger, who had recently deserted Labour for other political parties, jumping from one to another as her dreams of parliamentary influence disappeared, felt vindicated. The report was, she said, "damning" and, referring to the cynicism many had felt at her initial complaints, "at that moment people accused me and others of making it up, of it being a fabrication, and as we've seen in the report today, very, very clearly, it wasn't".[163] For those who actually took the trouble to read the report, it didn't seem as clear as Berger suggested.

It wasn't just the Labour Party - all sectors of civic society seemed to unite in welcoming and accepting the empty report and its total lack of anything significant. 'Hope not hate', ironically an anti-racism campaign group, said it was "unequivocal and damning". Chief Rabbi Ephraim Mirvis, saw it as a "historical nadir" for the party.[163]

Again, the interested nonpartisan observer might see this as symptomatic of the 'crisis' throughout – the vast disconnect in relation to what is claimed ("dark days"[163] and the like) and what has actually occurred (the release of a report flawed at its inception, unable or unwilling to define the parameters of what it was discussing and, ultimately, unable to find any evidence for what it claims to have proved).

In the wake of this report, Corbyn released the following statement on his Facebook site:

"Antisemitism is absolutely abhorrent, wrong and responsible for some of humanity's greatest crimes. As Leader of the Labour Party, I was always determined to eliminate all forms of racism and root out the cancer of antisemitism. I have campaigned in support of Jewish people and communities my entire life and I will continue to do so.

"The EHRC's report shows that when I became Labour leader in 2015, the Party's processes for handling complaints were not fit for purpose. Reform was then stalled by an obstructive party bureaucracy. But from 2018, Jennie Formby and a new NEC that supported my leadership made substantial improvements, making it much easier and swifter to remove anti-Semites. My team acted to speed up, not hinder the process.

"Anyone claiming there is no anti-Semitism in the Labour Party is wrong. Of course, there is, as there is throughout society, and sometimes it is voiced by people who think of themselves as on the left.

"Jewish members of our party and the wider community were right to expect us to deal with it, and I regret that it took longer to deliver that change than it should.

"One anti-Semite is one too many, but the scale of the problem was also dramatically overstated for political reasons by our opponents inside and outside the party, as well as by much of the media. That combination hurt Jewish people and must never be repeated.

"My sincere hope is that relations with Jewish communities can be rebuilt and those fears overcome. While I do not accept all of its findings, I trust its recommendations will be swiftly implemented to help move on from this period."[164]

For anyone familiar with him, this was classic Corbyn. A passionate anti-racist to his core, he concentrates on what he sees as the evils of anti-Semitism. As a man of diplomacy and conciliation, he hopes for better days in the now strained relations between some parts of the Jewish community and the party. What causes a furore, though, is his opinion that "the scale of the problem was also dramatically overstated for political reasons".[164] For Corbyn to utter such words was now akin to heresy, and the response was immediate. Within hours, refusing to retract his words, Corbyn - the hitherto leader of the party - was suspended!

In a bitter moment of being proved right, everything Chris Williamson and others had said had come to pass. The crisis, enabled by the party's insistence on apologising, appeasing and capitulating, had facilitated and emboldened the Zionist lobby and the neoliberal apologists. It was *they* who were behind the smear campaign and now threatened the party's very existence. The civil war between the left and right of the party broke into the open.

Now, as I write in February 2021, rather than draw a line in the sand over the issue, which Starmer seemingly wished to do, he appears to have done the opposite - the witch-hunt has never been more prominent in the public eye. And the controversy over Corbyn's continuing suspension from the party continues to grow in both scale and emotion, overwhelmingly from *outside* the Parliamentary Labour Party. The Socialist Campaign Group released a few ambiguous, wishy-washy faux solidarity statements to the media, but these so-called comrades of the left merely wrapped themselves in the tortured logic of expressing regret at Corbyn's suspension and, at the same time, conveyed a wish for him to issue yet another apology.

Arguably, all along, it has been these erstwhile supporters that have done the most damage to the left. It is much easier to deal with one's enemy when he or she is out in the open. Right-wing bully boys such as Ian Austin can easily be seen for who they are and their comments taken as such. But when people like John McDonnell express support, yet saddle it with further conditions, one would be better off without that support in the first place; their crocodile tears and misplaced concern serving only to give further credence to the lies and calumnies.

The mood amongst the senior leadership was unambiguous. Attending a Jewish Labour conference (which, coincidentally or not, was held on the same day as the International Day of Solidarity with the Palestinian People), Angela Rayner made a shocking announcement. "Our members need to get real about this," she stated. "If they don't think antisemitism is within the Labour Party and that there's no problems now, then there's really no place for them in the Labour Party." And, she went on, if they refused to accept the party line, then "If I have to suspend thousands and thousands of members, we will do that."[165]

This proposed direct intervention by the leadership into the party's internal complaints procedure, in clear contradiction of the recent EHRC report guidance[166] (the same report that Rayner and the rest of the leadership had reacted so slavishly to), seemed strangely undeserving of any comment, either internally by the Labour Party or by the media. Indeed, it was interesting that this particular piece of advice was now - after the right-wing faction had wrestled control of the levers of power from the left - being called into question.

The so-called Prince of Dark Arts, Peter Mandelson, stated "I'm worried about one thing. That is this recommended approach by the EHRC of an independent process." The NEC should remain, he suggested, in "ownership" of the process.[167] As stated before, I happen to agree with this position. Though it is striking that Mandelson had the right to refute and question the EHRC report, while figures on the left - such as Corbyn or Williamson - evidently could *not* without being labelled by all and sundry as anti-Semites. Rarely has hypocrisy been so stark.

If individual members or CLPs dared put their heads above the parapet - if only for a moment - they were immediately shut down, in an increasingly manic version of McCarthyism. Many of these instances would be touched upon briefly by the mainstream media as examples of the lunatic, anti-Semitic 'fringe' of Corbynistas who, stubbornly and irritatingly, refused to disappear. And it is worth looking at one such instance in more detail to see if we can come close to uncovering the 'truth' behind such claims.

After a meeting of her constituency, Nottingham East, on Friday 27th November 2020, Nadia Whittome - who purports to be on the left and is a member of the Socialist Campaign Group of Labour MPs - tweeted the following: "I am disappointed that a motion that was clearly out of order made its way up the agenda of the Nottingham East CLP meeting this evening which I attended. I take the EHRC report into Labour antisemitism very seriously, as should all our members given the pain caused to Jewish communities and that the report found the Labour Party to have broken the law. I would like to put on record my stated objection to the motion this evening. My objection was however overruled by the chair of the meeting. The atmosphere and tone of the meeting that proceeded was wholly unacceptable, leading to a Jewish member of the Labour Party feeling they had no choice but to leave the meeting."[168]

Interestingly, fellow participants at the meeting don't remember the evening in quite the same way. Indeed, so violently did they disagree with their MP's widely reported version of events, they released their own statement:

"We are members and delegates of Nottingham East CLP who were present at the meeting on Friday 27th November, held on Zoom. We wish to express our solidarity with our Chair, Louise Regan, who was suspended from the Labour Party within 15 minutes of the end of the meeting. We also wish to correct some misleading statements about the meeting currently circulating on social media – including that of our MP Nadia Whittome.

"There were different – strongly held - views expressed on whether we should hear the motion that called for Corbyn's reinstatement, the lifting of disciplinary measures from others for discussing the issues as well as for the removal of David Evans, General Secretary of the Labour Party. Nevertheless, the meeting was conducted throughout with respect for all speakers – with one notable exception, described below.

"All who wished to speak in the debate, both for and against, were given the opportunity to do so – and many did - such that our invited speaker volunteered to return at a future meeting. Several Jewish members gave their perspectives including many in favour. The leader of Nottingham City Council spoke against the motion being heard. Speakers also included our MP – who spoke twice against hearing the motion – despite not being a member of our CLP.

"At one point there were 58 participants, not all of whom were delegates able to vote. It is a credit to the Chair that the meeting was conducted fairly and respectfully with such a contentious issue. Members were asked to keep themselves muted unless they were called on to speak so that there was no sound interference when people were speaking. It should be noted that all the functions of the Zoom meeting, such as muting, were under the control of the Secretary and not the Chair.

"There was only one interruption during the meeting. This arose when one member stated that in his personal experience, he had never witnessed any anti-Semitism in any of our meetings. As he continued with his personal view, another member shouted out – in a manner that some found to be aggressive - that he himself had suffered personal, anti-Semitic abuse from the person speaking, who was taken aback and stated that this wasn't true; the Chair intervened and tried to calm things down. At this point the member who had interrupted declared that he no longer felt safe at the meeting and left.

"Members were stunned by this exchange, and the ensuing statement from the member saying he did not feel safe, followed by his exit. The atmosphere of the meeting immediately became tense and uncomfortable and many were very upset by it. It should be noted that there had been no anti-Semitic behaviour or language at the meeting. Several members then spoke of their concern for the member who had left and the Chair stated that she had reached out to him to check that he was ok. When all who wanted to speak had done so, a vote was proposed and seconded and the delegates voted on whether to hear the motion. This was carried overwhelmingly by 22 votes for to 9 against.

"The meeting then proceeded as per the agenda and on the suspension of standing orders to allow more time. The motion was presented to the meeting, with delegates voting that it should be under the condition of one person being allowed to speak in favour of the motion and one person against. The motion went to a vote and was carried by 23 votes in favour to 10 against.

"Additional concerns have arisen by the discovery that someone present was sending out live information – including members' names – to a journalist known to be hostile to Jeremy Corbyn and his supporters, who was live tweeting this information. It has also been noted that the member who left has changed his narrative on social media to stating that the member he accused had 'witnessed an anti-Semitic attack' on him rather than had attacked him personally.

"All Labour Party meetings should be conducted in a safe environment where all members' views can be expressed without fear of attack, either within or without the meeting.

"Louise Regan chaired our meeting in exemplary fashion throughout and we call for her reinstatement, along with all those who are facing disciplinary action for merely discussing issues of democracy and due process within the Party, as expressly affirmed in the EHRC report and in accordance with the Human Rights Act. Nadia joined others in saying thanks to Matt and Louise for the way they had conducted the meeting."[169]

Quite a different tale. And the background of the person suspended? Louise Regan, the chair in question, is a long-time activist on the left, well known in Labour Party circles regionally and from her prominent role inside the National Education Union (NEU). It was just over a year to the day that police were called to a Labour meeting (intent on discussing the selection of the new parliamentary candidate) when tempers boiled over concerning Louise Regan's exclusion - as the overwhelming, local Labour favourite - from the shortlist. And why was Regan not on the shortlist? Because, it is widely believed, of a smear from the tiny political group, Alliance for Workers' Liberty (AWL). And who participated and was ultimately the beneficiary of this smear? None other than Nadia Whittome. In fact, prior to the selection contest to pick the candidate, Nadia Whittome is said to have circulated a note to local Momentum members blackening Regan's name. The note falsely claimed that "she [Regan] only entered the left scene in 2014 after TU corruption allegations were made against her."[170]

Despite such underhand shenanigans and many other loud complaints around censorship, the Labour hierarchy continued to respond that they were merely trying to create a "safe space... [for] Jewish members".[171] The playground logic follows that anyone who challenges this is, de facto, denying this safe space. And so, in a chilling development for anyone who believed in a genuine democracy, by December of 2020, victory for the witch-hunt seemed almost complete. For, in a development straight out of a novel by Orwell or Kafka, it was now accepted and established that simply by *challenging* accusations of anti-Semitism it meant, in the eyes of British society, that you were an anti-Semite.

"People who live in an age of corruption are witty and slanderous; they know that there are other kinds of murder than by dagger and assault; they also know that whatever is well said is believed."

The Gay Science, Nietzsche

7 - With Friends Like These

With Corbyn's shock victory in Labour's September 2015 leadership election, the floodgates suddenly opened to unprecedented media scrutiny that had only one aim – to destroy Corbyn the man and, in so doing, damage and hopefully destroy the Labour left.

The left has, of course, always known criticism. It is a defining feature of its position in British society, that anyone claiming a political space for socialist ideas has always faced formidable opposition in the form of the status quo. Perhaps this story though - the story of the Labour Party anti-Semitism crisis as viewed by future historians - might be notable for the infighting and vitriol faced from those previously seen as allies.

I have already witnessed the shameful role that much of the Parliamentary Labour Party (PLP) played and continues to play. I have touched on the role of the media in amplifying Labour's internal strife; not surprising in that much of the British media acts as unofficial cheerleader to the Conservative Party (a position quite unique in Europe). That the abuse from the usual shady outlets like the *Daily Mail*, *The Sun*, *The Times*, et cetera would be loud and vulgar - not least because they helped manufacture it in the first place - could have been expected and was, dispiritingly, true to form. But arguably much more damaging was the role that previously favourable and fair-minded media organisations played during the whole 'crisis'.

The Guardian has, since its inception as *The Manchester Guardian* in 1821, generally been seen as the reputable home of British liberal values and, for much of its history, one of the very few (alongside that of the *Daily Mirror*) voices of support for Labour. So, when it turned into perhaps the most vociferous of those crying 'antisemitism', it proved - with the influence and inherited reputation from decades of journalism that was broadly sympathetic to the left - to be deeply damaging.

One can speculate as to the reasons why. David Cronin, a contributor to *The Guardian*, suggests - in an article he wrote for a pro-Palestinian website - that Jonathan Freedland's influential position at the newspaper has been of great significance, informed as he is by an unapologetic Zionism; a world view that has led him, in the past, to argue that the 'emptying' of 400 (Palestinian) villages in 1948 was justified on the grounds that the "creation of a Jewish state was a moral necessity".[172] This logical leap, for many of the commentariat, has very much granted Israel a Get Out of Jail Free card since its foundation.

Freedland's hostile and powerful position as editor of the 'Comment is free' section of the newspaper might have been more acceptable had it been leavened with dissenting opinions. Alas, there were few. And so, what this amounted to was article after article, all repeating the same, familiar narrative. To many a *Guardian* reader, such uniformity of opinion must have propounded circumstantial evidence that the truth was in play; after all, surely so many prominent journalists couldn't be wrong.

Repeatedly, however, journalists - trusted by the readership - came out with opinions on Israel/Palestine/anti-Semitism which were, at best, misleading and, at worst, cunningly mendacious. Helen Lewis, deputy editor of the *New Statesman*, is an example of this. Penning a 'Comment is free' article, on 1st April 2018 (under the watchful eye of Freedland), she wrote:

"An open letter defending Corbyn on Facebook last week, which attracted 2,000 likes, began by suggesting that the Labour leader must feel 'battered, bruised and damn near hopeless and helpless'.

"Those adjectives could also be applied to Berger, who has seen three men jailed for racist threats against her. 'Hitler was right,' read one of their comments, alongside a picture of the MP with a Star of David on her forehead. 'You better watch your back Jewish scum,' read another. The third called her an 'evil money-grabber' and Photoshopped her face on to a rat."[173]

The natural conclusion any reader would draw from this is that Labour supporters made the repugnant, anti-Semitic comments. The problem is...they didn't. Those found guilty of these particular anti-Semitic acts had absolutely nothing to do with Labour. For an experienced journalist like Lewis to be unaware of this salient and inconvenient fact hints at incompetence or impiety; perhaps a twisting of the truth to fit her narrative.

On 4th March 2019, John Harris, again utilising Freedland's 'Comment is free' agitprop, wrote an article entitled "The unanswered question: why do antisemites think Labour is the party for them?" which included an embedded video link of Berger listing the examples of anti-Semitism which she had been a victim of (alas, with no explanation that these were unrelated to Labour).[174]

Such propaganda kept on coming. On 2nd April 2019, Tracy-Ann Oberman, wrote:

"Worse was the misogyny and anti-Jewish abuse towards "Zio" Luciana Berger, at that point on Labour's newly formed frontbench. I assumed it was coming from the far right but shockingly it appeared to be coming from Labour Party members, too. My own party.

"I looked for a grownup to stamp hard on it. There was nobody. Seeing Berger's face grafted on to the body of a rat, a Star of David etched on to her head with the words #FilthyJewBitch, pushed me to stick my head above the parapet and call it out publicly. In doing so I became a target for trolling myself."[175]

In what was becoming a formulaic, but still shocking dereliction of duty (journalists espousing outright lies), anti-Semitism and its synonymousness with Labour Party members began to take on a whole new fallacious air.[176] But *The Guardian* was still *The Guardian* - the natural home of the influential and connected Labour voter. So, when a group of prominent British Jews wrote a letter of protest against the coverage the party had been receiving on this issue, it was *The Guardian* to whom they submitted it.

"You report (19 February [2019]) that a number of implacably anti-Corbyn MPs have left the Labour party alleging a failed "approach to dealing with antisemitism", with Luciana Berger criticising Labour for becoming 'sickeningly institutionally racist'.

"We are Jewish members and supporters of the Labour party concerned about the current rise of reactionary ideologies, including antisemitism, in Britain and elsewhere across Europe.

"We note the worrying growth of populist right-wing parties, encouraging racism, Islamophobia and antisemitism. In Britain the far right is whipping up these prejudices, a threat that requires a resolute and energetic response. But instead, we have seen a disproportionate focus on antisemitism on the left, which is abhorrent but relatively rare.

"We believe that the Labour party under the progressive leadership of Jeremy Corbyn is a crucial ally in the fight against bigotry and reaction. His lifetime record of campaigning for equality and human rights, including consistent support for initiatives against antisemitism, is formidable. His involvement strengthens this struggle.

"Labour governments introduced both the anti-racist and human rights legislation of the 20th century and the 2010 Equalities Act. A Labour government led by Jeremy Corbyn will be a powerful force to fight against racism, Islamophobia and antisemitism.

"It is in this context that we welcome the Labour party's endorsement of freedom of expression on Israel and on the rights of Palestinians. Labour is correct to recognise that while prejudice against Jewish people is deplorable, criticism of Israel's government and policies can and must be made.

"We urge all who wish to see an end to bigotry and racism, and who seek a more just society, to give their support to the Labour party."[177]

This letter, unambiguous in its opposition to anti-Semitism, but clear-sighted to the reality of the Labour Party and how it was being unfairly portrayed, was signed by hundreds of prominent British Jews, including academics. And this wasn't the first or last time that Jewish people had articulated their opposition to a witch-hunt taking place in their name.

On the 9th July 2019, *The Guardian* newspaper printed the following letter with regard to Chris Williamson:

"We the undersigned, all Jews, are writing in support of Chris Williamson and to register our dismay at the recent letter organised by Tom Watson, and signed by Parliamentary Labour Party and House of Lords members, calling for his suspension (Anger over return of MP who said Labour was 'too apologetic' over antisemitism, 28 June).

"Chris Williamson did not say that the party had been "too apologetic about antisemitism", as has been widely misreported. He correctly stated that the Labour Party has done more than any other party to combat the scourge of antisemitism and that, therefore, its stance should be less apologetic. Such attacks on Jeremy Corbyn's supporters aim to undermine not only the Labour Party's leadership but also all pro-Palestinian members.

"The mass media have ignored the huge support for Chris both within and beyond the Labour Party. Support that includes many Jews. The party needs people like him, with the energy and determination to fight for social justice. As anti-racist Jews, we regard Chris as our ally: he stands as we do with the oppressed rather than the oppressor. It should also be noted that he has a longer record of campaigning against racism and fascism than most of his detractors.

"The Chakrabarti report recommended that the party's disciplinary procedures respect due process, favour education over expulsion and promote a culture of free speech, yet this has been abandoned in practice. We ask the Labour Party to reinstate Chris Williamson and cease persecuting such members on false allegations of antisemitism."[178]

This letter was signed by over a hundred Jewish people from a wide swathe of society, including academics and members of the party. Prominent amongst them was internationally famous Jewish philosopher and writer Noam Chomsky. Chomsky had been unshrinking in his assessment of the Labour witch-hunt throughout. In an earlier email (5th July 2019), Chomsky had written this, referring to the comments Williamson had made at the Sheffield meeting:

"The way charges of anti-Semitism are being used in Britain to undermine the Corbyn-led Labour Party is not only a disgrace, but also - to put it simply - an insult to the memory of the victims of the Holocaust. The charges against Chris Williamson are a case in point. There is nothing even remotely anti-Semitic in his statement that Labour has "given too much ground" and "been too apologetic" in defending its record of addressing "the scourge of anti-Semitism" beyond that of any other party, as he himself had done, in public platforms and in the streets."[179]

Unfortunately, future historians will have a hard time finding the 9th July open letter as it was subsequently censored. *The Guardian* retracted it, just hours later, on the dubious grounds that minor errors allegedly existed in relation to some of the more obscure signatories.[180] Call it cynicism, but one doubts very much whether a similar sweep or zero-tolerance alertness is regularly exercised on the many letters that *The Guardian* receives.

This isn't the only time *The Guardian* has been guilty of outright censorship. Steve Bell, the famous cartoonist, worked for *The Guardian* for nearly 40 years. During that time, he become somewhat feared by his subjects, due to the biting satire of his sketches. In recent years, however, quite unusually, some of Bell's cartoons would not see the light of day.

Case in point in 2019, Bell had drawn Tom Watson as a witch finder pursuing Israeli President, Benjamin Netanyahu. In the cartoon, Watson is seen riding a horse. "An antisemitic trope? We will pursue it to the ends of the earth and beyond!!" Watson successfully captures his victims, Netanyahu, Trump and Johnson, only to realise his error at the end saying, "I'm awfully sorry! I thought you were members of the Labour Party!!"[181]

That this satire of the ongoing, overinflated witch-hunt should be blocked by *The Guardian* might not prompt bewilderment given their increasingly pusillanimous and politically correct stance. But Bell did not hold back his ire, emailing the editor:

"You said the "lawyers are concerned" but about what? It's not antisemitic nor is it libellous…I suspect the real cause is it contravenes some mysterious editorial line that has been drawn around the subject of antisemitism and the infernal subject of antisemitic tropes. In some ways this is even more worrying than the specious charges of antisemitism. Does The Guardian no longer tolerate content that runs counter to its editorial line?"[181]

The answer to this rhetorical question was becoming more evident by the day. And Bell was not - unlike so many others - going to be cowed into silence. Whether it was Ken Livingstone[182], wider Israeli issues[181], or Corbyn himself[183], Bell refused to see any of these - as *The Guardian* clearly wanted him to - as taboo or off-limits. Rarely, in fact, has a topic warranted such unalloyed attention, considering the very essence of free speech was at stake. It would come as no surprise that *The*

Guardian (now unrecognisable in part) chose 2020 as the right time to dispense with Steve Bell's services.[181]

Besides *The Guardian*, though, there were other strong voices on the left happy to collude with the anti-Semitism charade. Owen Jones, a journalist himself at the paper, had carved out a prominent media role wherein he could display his skills as an eloquent and combative speaker. The author of *Chavs*, *The Establishment* and - most recently - *This Land*, he had become a very influential and well-connected figure on the left.

In the chapter 'The Antisemitism crisis' from *This Land*, one finds an interesting account of Jones' thinking. He is, it must be said, clear-sighted in his assessment of the profoundly damaging role that the media have played in all this. He notes, for example, that in 2016 academics at the London School of Economics compiled a report examining a period of media coverage that spanned Corbyn's first few weeks as leader. Their findings, they wrote, illustrated "the ways in which the British press systematically delegitimised Jeremy Corbyn as a political leader" through a "process of vilification that went beyond the normal limits of fair debate and disagreement in a democracy."[184]

Fifty-seven per cent of news articles had a critical or antagonistic tone: "scathing, disingenuous, insulting or mocking". Thirty per cent of "news stories, editorials, commentaries, features or letters to the editor mock the leader of the opposition or scoff at his ideas, policies, history, his personal life – and, alarmingly, even his looks". Over half of all articles failed to include Corbyn's own views; another 22 per cent stripped them of context or distorted them. He was depicted as a comic caricature, referred to repeatedly as the "Jezster" or as "Mr Corbean", a reference to the slapstick sitcom character Mr Bean. "The Grinch [Jeremy Corbyn] cancels Christmas" and "refuses to issue festive message" declared *The Daily Telegraph*, four days after Corbyn had written a Christmas message for the *Daily Mirror*. He was also compared to Chairman Mao (on the grounds that his fairly bog-standard bike looked – according to *The Times*' news section, no less – like something the Great Leader might ride) and designated a terrorist sympathiser. He had "suspicious ties to terror groups", announced the

Daily Express, while *The Sun* called him a supporter of the IRA and "any heavily bearded jihadi mentals who long for the destruction of the West".[184]

Owen Jones further mentions the deeply damaging role internal malcontents played, listing notable incidents. This displayed itself in different ways - from personal abuse, to a media narrative of a Labour Party hostile to its leader. For example, in July 2016, when Corbyn was responding in Parliament to the Chilcot inquiry into the Iraq war, the then Labour MP Ian Austin yelled at him to "shut up", berating him as "a disgrace".[184]

At other times, Jones clearly identifies the manoeuvrings and stratagems initiated by the malcontents on the right, notably Hilary Benn and Margaret Hodge via their key roles as coup orchestrators. It is maddening, though, after seeing Jones correctly identify the issues around media portrayal, the role of Labour mischief-makers, and low levels of anti-Semitism in the party compared to others, that he goes on to blame the party leadership, Chris Williamson and elements of the membership as the guilty contingent in the whole 'crisis'.

Why Jones and prominent figures on the left do this is difficult to comprehend or fathom. His own book, for example, highlights a poll which finds that on average the "British public thought 34% of Labour members faced complaints of antisemitism"; a figure, in other words, over 300 times the reality! A discovery totally in line with Chris Williamson's conclusion that the whole affair was fabricated and overblown.[184]

The reader searches futilely for *why* Jones opts not to wholly attribute blame to the media and saboteurs for this crisis, but rather include the party itself in a complicit and culpable light. The answer to this conundrum might, perhaps, lie within the curious section devoted to Chris Williamson.

Rather than address Williamson's ideas themselves (the fundamental one being that the anti-Semitism 'crisis' was being purposely exaggerated in order to damage the party...something which Jones seemingly agrees with), a personal hatchet job takes place. Dismissing those on the left, who objected to Momentum's odd decision to run alongside the anti-Semitic bandwagon, as "cranks", Jones goes on to label Williamson "king of the cranks".[184]

There follows a snide account of Williamson's political journey to date, little of which seems relevant to the matter at hand. Williamson, Jones decrees, clearly seeing himself as the arbiter of all things 'left', yet "political history didn't place him on the left". Examples of this include Williamson's "support" for PFI while on Derby City Council and his backing of Ed Miliband rather than the "left" candidates of Diane Abbott or John McDonnell in the 2010 leadership elections. He was, Jones sweepingly declares, "a middle of the road 'soft left' MP who would tweet countdowns about how many days remained until a Miliband government would usher in "responsible capitalism". Williamson also supported war in Libya, Western airstrikes in Iraq in 2014, and refused to vote against Conservative workfare programmes in 2013.[184]

Williamson vehemently rejects this characterisation by Jones and has some harsh words of his own:

"My record speaks for itself. I fought Nazis on the streets and, as a young bricklayer, put my personal safety at risk by confronting casual racism on building sites in the 1970s when the fascist National Front were on the rise. I campaigned for Tony Benn to become the Labour Party's deputy leader and was arrested on picket lines and in protests against blood sports in the 1980s. I argued for and delivered municipal socialist policies when I was elected as a councillor in the 1990s and 2000s. And I moved heaven and earth to ensure the Labour Party moved on from New Labour in 2010, by campaigning for Ed Miliband, who was the only candidate capable of beating his brother. Without Ed Miliband, there would have been no Jeremy Corbyn, because it was Miliband who successfully changed the franchise for leadership elections from an electoral college, to a one-member-one-vote system. So, I won't take any lectures from him….nestled in his ivory tower at The Guardian…. The truth is that for the vast bulk of Jeremy's leadership, Owen Jones behaved like a fifth columnist."[69]

But even if Williamson *had* moved to the left, as Owen Jones asserted, it rather begs the question: So what? Surely for a figure on the left, as Jones claims to be, wasn't that precisely what he wanted - people being convinced by the force of the arguments in favour of socialism? Seemingly not, for in a sarcastic put-down, Jones states: "When he lost his seat in 2015, Williamson apparently re-invented himself as a revolutionary". Jones, the reader deduces, would have preferred it if Williamson was still 'soft left'.[184]

One thought persists: that Jones is simply trying to destroy Williamson's reputation. The heavy sarcasm and animosity behind these personal attacks seem to lead the reader into believing that Williamson's apparent 'reinvention' (to borrow Jones' logic) was an insincere Machiavellian move by an MP fawning to the new leader.

Jones goes on to list the greatest hits of the witch-hunters' spurious allegations about Williamson. Namely: "He retweeted a Holocaust denier writing about Venezuela", "tweeted his pleasure at meeting Miko Peled, an Israeli-American author who had said 'Jews have a reputation for being sleazy thieves'", and "tweeted in support of Gilad Atzmon". Once again, in a similar manner to the Labour Party itself, rather than be troubled by the *lack* of anti-Semitism in any of these instances, Jones narrowly lists them in a journalistic smokescreen; trying to establish by the sheer quantity of allegations - none of which stand up to any scrutiny - the very dubious 'pattern of behaviour' argument.[184]

Jones then - parading his journalistic credentials - raises the emotional stakes. The leadership, he claims, "pleaded" with Williamson to stop. But Williamson, Jones states, "refused to listen, lecturing them that 'if we keep running, they'll keep chasing' ". An interesting exercise here would be to remove the emotive verbs. Perhaps then, one could write:

when members of the leadership 'asked' Williamson to stop, he 'declined' to do so, saying that 'if we keep running, they'll keep chasing'. Having read Jones own accounts of the deeply damaging role of the Labour saboteurs and his reference to the facts behind the anti-Semitic smears, an engrossed reader might conclude that Williamson's suggestion to 'stop running' was worth a try. After all, the Labour Party's policy of appeasement and capitulation was blatantly failing. For reasons never entirely made clear though, Jones implies that Williamson's response was beyond the pale.[184]

Who knows the unadulterated truth behind these smears? Perhaps Jones, clearly frustrated at the whole issue (who isn't), casting around for someone to blame and, aware at the same time of the widespread criticism he and others had received on this, is motivated by something baser? For it is not in his interest, as a well-known figure on the left, to have someone of good standing in the movement, able to criticise his position on this. Someone like Williamson, in fact. So perhaps Jones felt it would better serve his interests by seeking to undermine and silence Williamson.

Jones finishes his convoluted and contradictory argument by reiterating "that the former leadership and the vast majority of Labour's membership abhor antisemitism" and then writes "the crisis led to months of media coverage, a prolonged drip-feed that helped fundamentally change the British public's sense of Corbynism from something positive to something poisonous and sinister." One agrees with all of this apart from the position of the words. For didn't 'months of media coverage' actually create or 'lead to the crisis'?[184]

Why Jones has a blind spot on this matter is not entirely clear. For it is only now that Jones claims *for the left to blame the media on this issue would be offensive as it removes personal agency*. One doesn't see Jones repeat this logic anywhere else. For example, in *Chavs*, he rightly criticises those who stigmatised the working class as the guilty party. It would be an entirely different book if he argued, as he does with his position on anti-Semitism, that it is 'the chavs', the working class, who must accept most of the blame as they are, in fact, 'in denial' about the vices they are guilty of (in their case, rather than anti-Semitism, this would be the litany of allegations the media often trot out – workshy, inefficient, and so on).

Instead, Jones, not surprisingly - as someone whose whole life revolves around the media - is seemingly obsessed by the optics of the issue; the truth relatively insignificant by comparison. For Jones, like so much of the commentariat, how the problem is *perceived* is king, regardless of the ensuing accuracy.

Jones argument would appear to boil down to this:

1. British Jews feel mistreated by the Labour Party.

2. Therefore, de facto, the Labour Party is anti-Semitic.

3. Consequently, the Labour Party must keep on continually apologising whenever a new allegation occurs, however tenuous.

4. Anyone who denies the validity of this argument is enabling anti-Semitism and is, therefore, an anti-Semite.

...to which one may counter: Throughout history, one sees groups of people, both small and large, with a false consciousness; the residents of Pendle or Salem possessed with the idea of witches in their midst; the mass of middle America convinced of Reds under the bed; 1980s Britain viewing the miner, fighting for his job, as 'the enemy within'. The list goes on. And to move forward – as Williamson pointed out in Sheffield - maybe the last thing one should do is keep apologising. For, to do so, merely feeds the sickness.

Jones' version of the truth on this matter is always pragmatic, always negotiable. Yet the acute tragedy in all of this is that he's probably correct on one important point: Maybe the majority of Jews *do* believe that the Labour Party is indeed anti-Semitic. It would scarcely be a shock given the overwhelmingly negative portrayal of the party over the last few years.

"One morning, upon awakening from agitated dreams, Gregor Samsa
found himself in his bed, transformed into an enormous insect."

Metamorphosis, Franz Kafka

Conclusion with Finkelstein

Jewish academic Norman Finkelstein knows *real* anti-Semitism when
he sees it, for it is, to him, a lived experience. His mother survived the
Warsaw ghetto, the Majdanek concentration camp and two slave labour
camps. His father survived the Warsaw ghetto and Auschwitz. Surely
it would be interesting to get his take on the British Labour Party anti-
Semitism 'crisis' – that some had called an 'existential threat' to British
Jewry. What did he have to say?

"Corbyn, he did not present a threat only to Israel and Israel's
supporters, he posed a threat to the whole British elite. Across the
board, from The Guardian to the Daily Mail, they all joined in the new
anti-Semitism campaign. Now that's unprecedented – the entire British
elite, during this whole completely contrived, fabricated, absurd and
obscene assault on this alleged Labour anti-Semitism, of which there is
exactly zero evidence, zero."[185]

So, what is the truth behind all this?

The 'truth' has, from time immemorial, been an elusive concept to
grasp, showing an alarming ability to wriggle out of one's fingers just
as one thinks it's firmly in your hand. Throughout history, battles have
been fought and lost in its name.

It seems easy now to determine where the truth lay in the battle between
Galileo and the Church. Of course, we say, referring to 'evidence' we
have usually gleaned from others, Galileo was in possession of the
truth, the holder of the conch, when he declared that it was the Earth
that revolved around the sun. And the Church was, courtesy of its claim
that the sun revolved around the Earth, false. This straightforward

deduction for us would not have been so easy for a native of Pisa in the 16th century, having to negotiate a different context of beliefs. For the 'truth', such as it is, is all too often only agreed upon when a socially acceptable consensus is arrived at.

We see these battles everywhere. For example, what is the truth with regard to Britain's colonial legacy? Is the 'truth' that Britain stripped the colonies of their wealth or laid the foundation for a functioning, modern civil society? Is the 'truth' of the French Revolution that it was a regrettable time of horror, bloodshed and anarchy or a new dawn for society, ushering in a future where notions such as liberty, equality and brotherhood seemed possible?

The 'truth' in these, as in so many matters, often depends upon which side of the political divide you are on. It is forever a very qualified quality, handed down from the future to the past by the fickle hands of posterity.

So, why bother? If objective truth is so hard to establish, so reliant on the fickle hands of chance, why should one waste one's time in such a fruitless hunt? I suppose Galileo provides the answer. For in sacrificing himself for the ideal of truth, he was fighting the battle that eventually resulted in history judging him the winner.

Similarly, in a different time and context with, admittedly, less serious ramifications, one hopes that the likes of Finkelstein and Chomsky and Chris Williamson will be seen in the future as having also waged an, at times, lonely and difficult battle.

So, what 'truth' are we *currently* able to gauge? Let us look briefly at some data in order to slowly dissect such a thing.

It should be acknowledged that, in modern Britain, anti-Semitism is a criminal offence. One can, and should, report it to the police.

Consequently, one would expect that any 'anti-Semitic crisis' in the Labour Party - at the level and over the timescale that has been alleged - would have resulted in a significant number of criminal convictions.

At this point in time then, one may ask, how many Labour MPs have been found guilty of committing an anti-Semitic crime? The answer is zero. For those frothing at the mouth regarding Ken Livingstone, Chris Williamson or Jeremy Corbyn, this must come as a surprise.

What about at the CLP level? Surely constituencies such as Berger's Liverpool Wavertree, seen by *The Guardian* and Berger as festering hotbeds of "anger, denial and prejudice", would have harboured CLP individuals ripe for committing such crimes?[186] The answer is, up to this point, not one Labour constituency member has been found guilty of committing an anti-Semitic crime.

Indeed, to find evidence of any anti-Semitic acts that have resulted in police action, anywhere in the country amongst Labour's half a million members, is difficult. There seems to have been only a handful of members scattered around who have faced criminal charges. And to my knowledge, at this moment in time, not one of them has been found guilty.

This surely is an improbable state of affairs, particularly for an issue that can easily be dealt with in court. Moreover, for such a 'crisis' to lack any evidence in relation to its existence, is quite an embarrassment. One looks in vain for the simple acknowledgement of this reality in either the party or the media.

Indeed, if we take the Labour Party's *in*correct definition of what anti-Semitism consists of, even then, despite Angela Rayner's claim that "thousands and thousands"[165] of members would be kicked out of the party over this issue, to date, only a relative few have been.[187] And, what is more, out of the hundreds of suspensions that have occurred, only a statistically small number have been upheld. For example, out of the 673 complaints of anti-Semitism during the peak witch-hunt year of April 2018 to January 2019, only 12 were upheld.[187] Many, if not all, of these expulsions are questionable, and some are subject to legal challenge.

The situation really is quite risible and absurd. Has there ever been a 'crisis' so undeserving of the name? For this distinct lack of evidence is not for want of trying, with one enquiry or report or investigation after another. For example, in October 2016, the House of Commons Home Affairs Committee released its own report on the matter. This authoritative and cross-party body concluded that:

"Despite significant press and public attention on the Labour Party, and a number of revelations regarding inappropriate social media content, there exists no reliable, empirical evidence to support the notion that there is a higher prevalence of antisemitic attitudes within the Labour Party than any other political party."[188]

Seeing as this is precisely the point that Chris Williamson, and (in a more watered-down version) Corbyn, were making, it begs the pertinent, yet preposterous question: Why weren't all the Labour members of the Home Affairs Committee similarly suspended?

The conclusions of the Home Affairs Committee were reinforced a year later when, in September 2017, the Institute for Jewish Policy research reported that:

"Levels of antisemitism among those on the left-wing of the political spectrum, including the far left, are indistinguishable from those found in the general population.... The most antisemitic group on the political spectrum consists of those who identify as very right wing: the presence of antisemitic attitudes in this group is 2 to 4 times higher compared to the general population."[189]

Not surprisingly, this report is seldom referred to anymore.

So where are we left? In my view, it seems self-evident that this has been the biggest non-story in British political history. A fabricated smear campaign comparable to the US McCarthyite witch-hunts of the 1950s.

And what, finally, will be the result of all this?

At this point, one is tempted to (in a similar fashion to the urban myth about the Chinese politician being asked about the effects of the French Revolution) respond with "It is too soon to tell"[190]. One hopes that - at least for the sake of Britain's Jewish community (outrageously being used as a political football in the most reprehensible way) - 'anti-Semitism' will cease being the go-to term for those on the right seeking to attack and undermine the left.

In the short to medium term, the discussion around the whole vital issue of Israel/Palestine has been made more difficult, with wide swathes of the political left being warned off this topic by the actions of the last few years. Perhaps a single tweet, relatively insignificant in itself, gives a clue as to the faux sensitivity or foolishness which still exists. On 29th November 2020, Jeremy Corbyn, on the International Day of Solidarity with the Palestinian People, tweeted: "Solidarity with the Palestinian people"[191]. Uncontroversial, one might think. Redbridge Labour Party, however, took it upon themselves to reply as follows: "Your solidarity is not for them. It is simply anti-Jewish. Of all the conflicts in the world the one that is the least harmful and where one side, Israel, has never instigated war or attacks. Antisemitism is rife thanks to you."[192]

Wide swathes of the Labour Party had, it seemed, taken the approach much desired by the Netanyahu leadership; to directly link any outward support for Palestine with being an anti-Semite!

The effect in the short term of weakening the British left through this manufactured diversion has been obvious. From a rare point of unity, under Corbyn's leadership, the left - as so often before - has splintered into varied, competing groups. It was ever thus, but, this time, those looking to apportion blame would be best directed to the reactionary right within the party and its slavish followers in wider society. For those on the left, this will go down in infamy and will long be remembered. The disgraceful use of the term 'anti-Semitism', exploited mainly by people with no bona fide interest in genuine prejudice, to destroy and vilify those very same people who had always stood against all forms of racism is truly deplorable. And all this done with no thought for the British Jewish community, using a people's emotions and fears for their own political ambitions. It is hard to forgive. And the left *will* remember.

Would Williamson's approach have worked? Should the Labour Party have agreed with him, not "to back off", not to be "apologetic", not to "give ground"?[106]

It is perhaps easy to say, after three years of turmoil, sackings, constant bad press, division within the Jewish community, divisions within the Labour Party, that it couldn't have been any worse! In reality, however, we will never know how such a tactic would have played out. It is tempting to imagine, though, that a firmer line held by Labour, with a more rational and higher standard of what constituted 'anti-Semitism', would have undermined a lot of the criticisms. Yes, the saboteurs may have continued to howl in outrage, with their media mouthpieces faithfully picking up their pleas. But, if Labour had consistently played a flat bat to these, over time, one hopes that the litany of false allegations would have been exposed for the lies they are. To paraphrase the great miners' leader, Mick McGahey, if the Labour Party hadn't run, it wouldn't have been chased.

It is also tempting to think, that if the party had taken Williamson's line, the result would have been to avoid a needless culture war, thus exposing the bad faith actors within the party for what they are. This, over time, would more likely have reassured the Jewish community regarding any pressing concerns. Continually preaching to the choir, however, with such hysterical and false accusations has stoked a climate of fear and hysteria. For those Jewish Labour voters who *hadn't* followed every move, in seeing numerous headlines about an 'existential threat', it would have been very hard not to absorb some of this fear.

So, where does this leave us – especially in a post-truth dystopia where it is now sufficient to merely state that a candidate is anti-Semitic for the damage to be done? For the lazy or unscrupulous journalist, the fact that one can assert such a claim and confidently expect not to be on the receiving end of any criticism makes one's life much easier. The politicians and journalists involved in this sorry saga have, in truth, been able to do exactly this for many years now. Of course, when one has reached a position when the term 'anti-Semitic' can be used without context or rationale or explanation, one is in a dangerous place. Words are weaponised, ready to be deployed at a moment's notice, resulting in incalculable damage.

What of the future? Will this term continue to be used? Will other careers be destroyed like Williamson's has? Or will multiple brave voices contest this and finally break through? For this to work, the left must stay united and be prepared to call out untruths where they see them without fear or favour. For falsehoods do damage to the very cause they feign to represent. The left must never countenance *genuine* anti-Semitism. But to continually use such a term risks delegitimising and politicising it - a tragedy that every right-thinking person should oppose.

This could be a straightforward task if the will is there. The left, yes, must consistently call out genuine anti-Semitism when it sees it. Those who peddle myths and conspiracies of a world bankrolled by a Jewish elite, say, should be given short shrift. But conversely, with one voice, we should call out lies when we see them. And not apologise when we have done nothing wrong. Finally…stand in solidarity, as always, with those who suffer and those who are attacked.

AFTERWORD - by Chris Williamson

When Lee Garratt approached me to ask for my assistance with his research for this book, I was happy to agree. The topic he has covered is particularly important, because it deals with the biggest tragedy of the Corbyn years, which was the capitulation to apartheid apologists.

At the end of Jeremy Corbyn's victory speech when he was overwhelmingly elected Labour leader in September 2015, he said: "*Things can, and they will change.*"[193] But despite overseeing more than four turbulent years as leader of the Labour Party, things didn't change in the way Jeremy was expecting.

The hope and enthusiasm that he brought to his role as Labour leader was met with unparalleled hostility from the Parliamentary Labour Party and the party's bureaucracy. But as this book highlights, it was his response to the Zionist movement that was to be his undoing. The Israel lobby was alarmed that a veteran pro-Palestinian activist and critic of the state of Israel was now the leader of the official opposition and a potential future prime minister.

The Corbyn project was woefully ill-prepared to take on the range of powerful vested interests that ultimately brought him down. Jeremy's response to the most relentless of those opponents, namely the Israel lobby, was the most significant contributing factor to his downfall. They were responsible for manufacturing the bogus anti-Semitism crisis in Labour and were gloating after the 2019 election defeat. For example, Joe Glasman, from the so-called 'Campaign Against Antisemitism', even recorded a video in which he referred to the surge in support for Jeremy's ideas as a "*rancid Tony Benn revival act*" and said: "*The beast is slain...we defeated him*".[194] The day after the election, Marie van der Zyl, president of the Board of Deputies of British Jews, said, "*history will not look kindly on Jeremy Corbyn's leadership of the Labour Party.*"[195]

It could have all been so different. This book chronicles how anti-Semitism was weaponised to destabilise and defeat Jeremy. The popular movement he inspired represented the biggest challenge to the status quo since Tony Benn was in his pomp at the beginning of the 1980s. The prospect of genuine radical change in this country was once again a real possibility, and that sent a shiver down the spine of the vested interests that members elected him to challenge.

I was Jeremy's most outspoken supporter in the House of Commons, which made me a target for disgruntled Labour MPs, mischief-making bureaucrats and Zionists. Consequently, I expected trouble, but I never anticipated just how serious that trouble would turn out to be. I certainly didn't expect to be forced out of the party to which I had devoted my entire adult life.

But Tony Benn's words have been ringing in my ears since the Corbyn project was vanquished inside the Labour Party. Tragically, the strategic errors by key figures in the movement meant that it was as much a case of self-immolation as it was a defeat inflicted by fifth columnists, right-wing reactionaries and saboteurs.

Speaking some years after he had left parliament so he could have "*more time to devote to politics*", Tony said: "*The older I get the more I realise that every single generation has to fight the same battles again and again and again.*"[196]

This rousing statement perfectly encapsulates my feelings about how we come to terms with the collapse of Corbynism within the Labour Party and where we go from here. Lee Garratt's book provides an invaluable insight into the strategies that will be deployed to destroy any serious future attempt to establish an anti-imperialist socialist alternative to the current political consensus. Such a prospect might seem like an impossible pipe dream now, in view of what happened from September 2015 when Jeremy was elected Labour leader, to his suspension from the party five years later.

But what Jeremy Corbyn demonstrated is that there is a massive appetite for an alternative to the unfettered corporate capitalism that has dominated since Labour chancellor, Denis Healey, opened the door to neoliberalism in 1976. Healey was panic-stricken by currency speculators and his failure of nerve led him to capitulate to them, rather than using the economic instruments at his disposal to take them on and defeat them. Healey's timidity is comparable to Jeremy's failure to mobilise the grassroots movement he had inspired. With their support, he could have taken on and defeated the opponents of socialism and anti-imperialism who inhabit the upper echelons of the Labour Party.

But the hundreds of thousands of people who were motivated by Jeremy's message have not disappeared into the ether. The socialist spirit that they epitomised lay dormant for 30 years until Jeremy succeeded in getting onto the ballot paper for the Labour leadership in the summer of 2015. At last, we had someone we could get behind who articulated a socialist anti-imperialist vision. Tony Blair and New Labour had killed the passion that was such a feature of the Labour Party I joined in 1976, six months before the rot set in with Healey's ill-considered IMF loan application. Neil Kinnock, who was the Labour leader for nine years, is responsible for creating the environment where the New Labour monster could evolve. He was obsessed with wooing corporate capitalism and expelling socialists from the Labour Party.

When he stepped down as leader, after losing the 1992 general election, John Smith took over until his untimely death in May 1994. Smith had rejected efforts by the New Labour wannabes to jettison Labour's commitment to socialism that was contained in clause iv of the party's constitution. But when Blair won the leadership later that year, he could not wait to finish the job Kinnock had started.

Those of us who stuck with the party had to content ourselves with crumbs from the table. One of those crumbs was Ed Miliband, who promised to turn the page on New Labour. In his first speech as leader to the Labour Party conference, he said: "*We must never again give the impression that we know the price of everything and the value of nothing.*"[197] And unlike previous Labour leaders, he was prepared to stand up to the Israel lobby. But the promise of that early crumb turned to dust. The party went into the 2015 election offering austerity-lite to appeal to Tories and using right-wing anti-immigration rhetoric in a desperate attempt to neutralise UKIP. It was a foolhardy and catastrophic strategy and resulted in even fewer Labour MPs being returned to parliament than in 2010. I lost my seat in Derby North by just 41 votes in 2015, even though I distanced myself from Labour's cuts agenda and the anti-immigration stance being promoted by Miliband, Ed Balls and Harriet Harman.

Jeremy Corbyn was a huge breath of fresh air that revitalised a moribund party with new ideas that signified an unapologetic commitment to socialism and opposition to imperialism. Opinion polls showed that the policies Jeremy was advocating were popular[198] and when Gyles Brandreth went looking for secret socialists in the Home Counties he found people were surprisingly receptive to Jeremy's policies.[199] In an item he recorded for BBC's 'The One Show' in 2016, he asked locals in Guildford if they wanted tuition fees scrapped, rail renationalised, NHS and social care integrated, privatisation ended, rent controls imposed and higher taxes on the wealthy. All the respondents approved of the policies.

How did it all go so wrong when the policies were popular, and the party had grown to become the largest in Europe?[200] This book offers an explanation. The biggest single factor was the leadership's repeated attempts to appease the Israel lobby. But if history teaches us anything, it is that appeasement does not work. I told Jeremy he had nothing to apologise for. I pleaded with the Socialist Campaign Group of Labour MPs to draw a line in the sand and start fighting back. But all my exhortations fell on deaf ears.

The Parliamentary Labour Party (PLP) was incredibly exercised by the combination of the growth in grassroots activists and my campaign to democratise the party, which would have made Labour MPs accountable to members. That accountability would have included subjecting them to an endorsement process between every election. For Labour MPs sitting on huge majorities, they essentially have a job for life, no matter how far they stray from socialist values. Most of them were therefore desperate to derail the desire to deepen democracy that was being expressed by Labour activists in every constituency in the country.

Meanwhile, the pro-Israel Zionist lobby was apoplectic that the leader of the official opposition in parliament was a longstanding critic of Israel and supporter of the Palestinian people. After the huge surge in the vote for Labour at the 2017 general election there was now a very real possibility that Jeremy would be the next UK prime minister. This was intolerable to the Israeli state, and their ambassador, Mark Regev, worked closely with the Jewish Labour Movement (JLM)[201] who refused to campaign to make Jeremy prime minister in 2019.[202] So, Lee was quite right to refer to the Al Jazeera documentary that was broadcast in early 2017, which exposed their insidious methods.[147] Jeremy called for an inquiry into the activities of the Israeli embassy officer who was caught on tape by the Al Jazeera investigation discussing a plot to "take down"[203] British politicians. In an open letter to the prime minister at the time, Theresa May, he described the actions of the Israeli embassy official, Shai Masot, as an "*improper interference in this country's democratic process,*" and said it was "*clearly a national security issue.*"[203] However, no action was ever taken, and Jeremy never raised the issue again.

These two groups – the PLP, along with their supporters in the party's bureaucracy and the Israel lobby – embarked on a pincer movement to strangle the Corbyn project. The anti-Semitism smears were intensified against Jeremy and his supporters and I was at the top of their hit list.

There was never any recognition that the capitulation strategy was making matters worse. Jeremy's advisers seemed to have the collective memory of a goldfish, and rather than drawing a line in the sand, the Socialist Campaign Group chose to bury their heads in it. Both failed to see, or opted to ignore, the blindingly obvious fact that the Israel lobby would not be satisfied until Jeremy was finally ousted. This was what the right-wing dominated PLP wanted too. Some Labour MPs are committed Zionists, including Sir Keir Starmer, who says he supports Zionism "*without qualification*"[204], while others wanted Jeremy out for different reasons. All of them enthusiastically weaponised anti-

Semitism and were eagerly aided and abetted by the corporate media in doing so.

The consequence of this failure to face down those hostile factions has handed the Labour Party over to the vested interests who want to maintain the economic and foreign policy status quo. The inevitable outcome of those goldfish memories and that ostrich-like behaviour was the disastrous 2019 general election result, and the subsequent events that unfolded following the publication of the EHRC report.

But despite the Corbyn project's deeply disappointing denouement, it did provide a salutary lesson to the labour movement, by demonstrating the impossibility of turning the Labour Party into a vehicle for socialism and anti-imperialism. Any hope of the left wresting control of the Labour Party evaporated when Jeremy announced his decision to step down as leader after losing the last general election.

The question now is what next? Representative democracy is in crisis. The MPs in parliament neither reflect nor represent the people who elect them. Well-endowed lobbies have far more influence over legislation than the public at large. Yet despite these obvious failings that have resulted in soaring poverty and inequality at home, and instability and human rights abuses around the world, the corporate media continues to manufacture consent for this broken system.

When the Marxist philosopher, Antonio Gramsci, said "*The crisis consists precisely in the fact that the old is dying and the new cannot be born; in this interregnum a great variety of morbid symptoms appear*"[205], he could have been describing the situation we are facing today. Socialists and anti-imperialists therefore have an obligation to find common cause to help the new to be born and reverse the morbid symptoms we are already witnessing, like the rise of the far right.

Raising political consciousness is crucial to creating the conditions for the new to be born and that is already happening organically. Grassroots movements are being created, with Black Lives Matter probably the most significant to date. Others are also being established such as Acorn[206], Palestine Action[207] and Resist: Movement for a People's Party[208] that are challenging modern-day orthodoxies. Local activism is on the increase and that needs to be nurtured and encouraged.

So, in spite of the setbacks and failure to fulfil the potential of the Corbyn project, I am optimistic about the future. The Zionist lobby overreached itself and many more people are aware of its pernicious and vindictive tactics. The situation in Palestine has also reached a much wider audience and now the Boycott, Divestment, Sanctions (BDS) campaign is more widely known. Lee Garratt has provided an invaluable insight into how not to respond to bad faith actors. When a new movement rises from the ashes of the Corbyn project, as it surely will, this book will be essential reading to ensure the same mistakes are not repeated.

APPENDIX I:
Witch-Hunt Case Study 1

Naomi Wimborne-Idrissi

The Jewish Vice Chair of Chingford and Woodford Green Labour Party.

At an online meeting of her CLP on the 30th November 2020, in response to discourse on the Labour Party banning the discussion of pro-Corbyn motions or the EHRC report, Ms Wimborne-Idrissi said:

"The idea – and I have to mention it – the idea that Jewish people require for their comfort that whole swathes of subjects should not be debated by the membership of this party is insulting to Jewish people. And I know there are some Jews in this meeting who will say "No No I think it's wonderful." This is a dangerous road. Do we really want us Jewish members to be seen as gatekeepers – as people who prevent others from discussing issues of importance? This is serious stuff comrades."[209]

Returning to the issue of some members apparently being discomfited by the conversation, she went on to state that it was people like herself, the left, who now "feel uncomfortable. I feel bloody uncomfortable seeing damned good comrades and friends of mine being suspended from the party for doing nothing more than trying to discuss the questions which led to Jeremy Corbyn's *un*just suspension - we know it was unjust because he was readmitted - and then the question of the whip being taken from him, which is almost certainly unconstitutional in the party."[209]

After the reports of Idrissi's comments were leaked and reported in the *Jewish Chronicle*, she was suspended from the party on the 3rd December 2020, "pending an investigation".[210]

APPENDIX II:
Witch-Hunt Case Study 2

Moshé Machover

Jewish. Born in Tel Aviv in 1936.

A founder of Matzpen, the Israeli socialist organization, in 1962.

Professor of Mathematics and Philosophy.

Machover was suspended from the Labour Party in 2017 (on the grounds of anti-Semitism) after an article he wrote entitled 'Anti-Zionism does not equal anti-Semitism.'[211]

His suspension was initiated by Sam Matthews of the GLU (later to receive prominence in the Panorama programme and the leaked internal report).[212] Well-known scholar then Labour MP, John Mann, responding in his typical 'reasonable' way, claimed that Labour Party Marxists should be "thrown out of the party, every single one of them", adding that the "scurrilous publication [responsible, *Weekly Worker*,] which contains anti-Semitic material, is good only for the recycling bin."[211]

In response to his suspension, Machover was his usual forthright self. Amongst other points he made - in an interview which debunked the whole witch-hunt in an admirably clear fashion – he stated:

"They had already decided to go on the attack internationally, using this 'dirty bomb' tactic of labelling as 'anti-Semitic' any criticism of Zionism and its colonisation project.

"In the UK, they found useful fools in the form of the Labour right wing. The Israeli state's propaganda tactic of smearing all criticism of itself as anti-Jewish coincided with the Labour...right's need to discredit Corbyn and the left of the party.

"Now Corbyn has plenty of enemies - both inside and outside the party! So this smear tactic was eagerly seized upon - including by people who care absolutely *nothing* about the issues of Israel-Palestine, the Jews, Zionism and all these important questions. They are totally cynical in their use of these issues. As Chris Williamson's phrase goes, the Labour right 'weaponised' the sensitive and complex issue of anti-Semitism for the sake of narrow, factional advantage against a left in the Labour Party that was growing and threatening to overwhelm them.

"It's a dirty war."[213]

Machover's suspension was eventually overturned following an outcry from members who pointed out the problem of expelling well-known Jewish intellectuals in a crusade to, ermm, fight anti-Semitism.[212]

Suspension 2:

Machover was suspended for a second time on the 3rd December 2020 after receiving a 20-page letter cataloguing a variety of supposed offences. Machover however - not one to suffer fools - responded by saying he wouldn't be engaging with Labour's disciplinary process, describing the letter as "full of lies" and "full of shit". "I refuse to play this game," Machover said in an email to his supporters. "I literally have no case to answer."[214]

As an example of the nature of the convoluted and bogus allegations he faced, one of the examples included was the grievous sin of attending a Palestinian solidarity demonstration against an Israeli film festival.[214]

APPENDIX III:
Motions moved or supported by Corbyn pertaining to anti-Semitism

Corbyn organised the Apr. 1977 defence of Jewish populated Wood Green from a Neo-Nazi march

EDM3933 7 Nov. 1990: Corbyn signs motion condemning the rise of antisemitism

EDM634, 11 Apr. 2000: Jeremy Corbyn signs motion condemning David Irving for being a Holocaust Denier

EDM1124, 6 Nov. 2000: Jeremy Corbyn praised the 'British Schindler', Bill Barazetti, for his WW2 Kindertransport

EDM742, 28 Jan. 2002: Jeremy Corbyn signs motion praising football clubs for commemorating Holocaust Day

EDM1233 30 Apr. 2002: Corbyn was a primary sponsor on a motion condemning antisemitism

11 May 2002: Jeremy led a clean-up of Finsbury Park Synagogue after an anti-Semitic attack

EDM1691, 23 July 2002: Corbyn condemned attacks on a synagogue in Swansea

EDM123 26 Nov. 2003: Corbyn officially condemns attacks on two Istanbul synagogues

EDM298, 16 Dec. 2003: Jeremy Corbyn signs motion commemorating International Holocaust Day

2004: Jeremy condemned news that anti-Semitic hate crimes had risen for yet another year

EDM461, 21 Jan. 2004: Jeremy Corbyn condemned the French government's moves to ban the Jewish Kippa in French Schools

EDM717, 26 Feb. 2004: Jeremy signed a motion praising Simon Wiesenthal for bringing Nazi perpetrators of the Holocaust to justice

EDM1613, 8 Sept. 2004: Corbyn co-sponsored a bill expressing fears for the future of the United Synagogue Pension Scheme

EDM1699, 11 Oct. 2004: Jeremy Corbyn condemned arbitrary attacks on civilians in Israel and Palestine

EDM482, 12 Jan. 2005: Jeremy Corbyn signs a motion commemorating International Holocaust Day

EDM343, 16 June 2005: Jeremy condemned the desecration of a Jewish cemetery in east London

EDM1343, 11 Jan. 2006: Jeremy Corbyn signs a motion commemorating International Holocaust Day

EDM1774, 8 Mar. 2006: Jeremy Corbyn led condemnations of an Iranian magazine soliciting cartoons about the Holocaust

EDM1267, 16 Apr. 2006: Jeremy Corbyn condemned Bryan Ferry for anti-Semitic remarks

EDM2414, 26 June 2006: Jeremy Corbyn praised British war veterans for their efforts to combat the Holocaust

EDM2705, 10 Oct. 2006: Jeremy signed a motion marking the 70th anniversary of Cable Street

EDM271, 14 Nov. 2007: Jeremy co-sponsored a motion lamenting the poverty and social exclusion East London Jews suffered

EDM153, 12 May 2008: Corbyn praised the efforts of the Jews in the Warsaw Ghetto during the uprising of 1944

EDM2350, 27 Oct 2008: Jeremy Corbyn signs a motion marking the 70th anniversary of the horrors of the holocaust

EDM173, 8 Dec. 2008: Jeremy condemned the Press Complaints Commission for refusing to sanction The Times for antisemitism

EDM461, 14 Jan. 2009: Jeremy Corbyn condemned a wave of recent anti-Semitic incidents targeted

EDM605, 27 Jan. 2009: Corbyn signed John Mann's motion condemning antisemitism on university campuses

EDM917 26 Feb. 2009: Jeremy signs a motion condemning antisemitism on the internet

EDM1175 24 Mar. 2009: Corbyn signs a motion praising the heroism of British Jews during Holocaust

EDM337, 2 Dec. 2009: Jeremy Condemned Iran's treatment of Jewish minorities in Iran

EDM850 9 Feb. 2010: Jeremy joins in calls for Facebook to do more to fight antisemitism

EDM891: 22 Feb 2010: Corbyn co-sponsors a motion calling for Yemen's Jews to be given refugee status to the UK

EDM908 27 Oct. 2010: Corbyn praises work of late Israeli PM in his pursuit of a two-state solution

EDM1360, 27 Jan. 2011: Corbyn co-sponsored a motion praising the 'never again for anyone initiative'

EDM1527, 3 Mar. 2011: Corbyn backed Ian Paisley's motion condemning the anti-Semitic remarks of Dior's lead fashion designer

EDM2870, 14 Mar. 2012: Jeremy Corbyn condemned the sale of Nazi memorabilia at an auction in Bristol

EDM2866, 14 Mar 2012: Jeremy Corbyn co-sponsored a bill condemning the rise of antisemitism in Lithuania

EDM2899, 20 Mar. 2012, Jeremy Corbyn condemned a terrorist attack on a Jewish school in Toulouse

EDM168, 12 June 2012, Jeremy co-sponsored a motion condemning anti-Semitic attacks during EURO 2012 in Poland

EDM 195 13 June 2012: Jeremy attacks BBC for cutting Jewish programmes from its schedule

EDM 1133 1 Mar 2013: Corbyn joins a chorus of calls condemning antisemitism in sport

1 Oct. 2013: Corbyn was one of the few MPs who defended Ralph Miliband from Daily Mail antisemitism

EDM 932 9 Jan 2014: Jeremy praises Holocaust Memorial's work on antisemitism education

EDM 165 22 June 2015: Jeremy condemns a Neo-Nazi rally planned for a Jewish area of London

Sat 4 July 2015: Jeremy co-planned a counter-fascist demo in defence of Jewish residents at Golders Green. The march was re-routed

18 Nov. 2015, Corbyn used one of his first PMQs to challenge Cameron to do more on antisemitism

9 Oct 2016: Corbyn, close to tears, leads commemoration of the Battle of Cable Street

3 Dec. 2016: Corbyn visits Terezin Concentration Camp to commemorate Holocaust victims

In 2017-19 Jeremy introduced 20 new measures to combat antisemitism in the Labour Party

The Labour Party

Head Office
Southside, 105 Victoria Street, London SW1E 6QT
Labour Central, Kings Manor,
Newcastle Upon Tyne NE1 6PA
0345 092 2299 | labour.org.uk/contact

Mr Christopher Williamson
[address removed]

27 February 2019

REF: A168248

Dear Mr Williamson,

Notice of administrative suspension from holding office or representing the Labour Party

Allegations that you may have been involved in a breach of Labour Party rules have been brought to the attention of national officers of the Party. These allegations relate to a series of actions which have brought the Party into disrepute, and which may constitute a breach of Chapter 2 Clause 2.I.8. It is important that these allegations are investigated and the NEC will be asked to authorise a full report to be drawn up with recommendations for disciplinary action if appropriate.

A large number of complaints have been received about your conduct. Several of these, if taken as an isolated incident, may have resulted in no action, a reminder of values or an investigation that might have resulted in a potential first written warning.

However, taken together they add up to a pattern of behaviour that may bring the party into disrepute. I have personally spoken to you about the damaging effect of this pattern of behaviour on Jewish communities and on the Labour Party's efforts to rebuild trust with those communities. Your position as a Member of Parliament places an even greater expectation of the standard of behaviour that you should meet.

The pattern of behaviour has included allegations of campaigning in favour of members who have been formally disciplined by the Party for antisemitism; failing to delete retweeted material from a holocaust denier, even after it was pointed out to you that the retweeted account belonged to an individual with such unacceptable views; tweeting and signing petitions in support of an individual who a Labour council had refused to allow to perform in their premises because of the individual's history of antisemitism; sharing platforms and giving public praise to people with a history of allegations of antisemitism against them; publicly attacking the Board of Deputies of British Jews, just hours after a synagogue suffered a mass shooting in the United States, which caused deep fear among every Jewish household. A range of other allegations have also been made against you, but the list above is sufficient for the time being to indicate the pattern of behaviour to which I refer.

I therefore write to give you formal notice that it has been determined that the powers given to the NEC under Chapter 6 Clause I.1.A of the Party's rules should be invoked to suspend you from office or representation of the Party*, pending the outcome of an internal Party investigation. The administrative suspension means that you cannot attend any Party meetings including Annual Conference and meetings of the Parliamentary Labour Party, and you cannot be considered for selection as a candidate to represent the Labour Party at an election at any level**.

In view of the urgency to protect the Party's reputation in the present situation it has been determined to use powers under Chapter 1 Clause VIII.5 of the rules to impose this suspension forthwith, subject to the approval of the next meeting of the NEC.

An Investigating Officer will be in further communication with you to arrange conduct of the Party's investigation. You will be contacted in due course with details as to how the investigation will proceed. All evidence of allegations will be presented to you, and you will be given an opportunity to put your explanation for the evidence. Please quote your membership number A168248 on all correspondence.

The Labour Party's investigation process operates confidentially. That is vital to ensure fairness to you and the complainant, and to protect the rights of all concerned under the Data Protection Act 2018. I must therefore ask you to ensure that you keep all information and correspondence relating to this investigation private, and that you do not share it with third parties or the media (including social media). That includes any information you receive from the Party identifying the name of the person who has made a complaint about you, any witnesses, the allegations against you, and the names of Party staff dealing with the matter. If you fail to do so, the Party reserves the right to take action to protect confidentiality, and you may be liable to disciplinary action for breach of the Party's rules. The Party will not share information about the case publicly unless, as a result of a breach of confidentially, it becomes necessary to correct inaccurate reports. In that case we will only release the minimum information necessary to make the correction. **The Party may also disclose information in order to comply with its safeguarding obligations.**

The Party would like to make clear that there is support available to you while this matter is being investigated. There are a number of organisations available who can offer support for your wellbeing:

You can contact your **GP** who can help you access support for your mental health and wellbeing.

The Samaritans are available 24/7 – They offer a safe place for anyone to talk any time they like, in their own way – about whatever's getting to them. Telephone **116 123.**

Citizens Advice - Provide free, confidential and impartial advice. Their goal is to help everyone find a way forward, whatever problem they face. People go to the Citizens Advice Bureau with all sorts of issues. They may have money, benefit, housing or employment problems. They may be facing a crisis, or just considering their options. **https://www.citizensadvice.org.uk/**

If you have questions about the investigation process please contact the Investigating Officer, whose details will are included in this letter. If you have any questions regarding support available from the party please call the **Safeguarding Unit on 0207 783 1134 Mon – Fri 9:30 – 4:30.**

It is hoped you will offer your full co-operation to the Party in resolving this matter.

Yours sincerely

Jennie Formby

General Secretary

The Labour Party

APPENDIX V:
Chris Williamson's response

I set out my responses to the Investigation Questions below. I confirm
I have made a Data Subject Access Request to secure copies of the
'large number of complaints' that are referred to in your letter dated 27
February 2019. These 'complaints' allegedly 'add up to a pattern of
behaviour that may bring the [Labour] Party (the Party) into disrepute.'
Without sight of these, I am precluded from fully defending the
allegations against me, or assessing their validity and veracity. I have
co-operated and respond as fully as possible based on the limited
information that has been provided.

I have been a Labour Party member for a continuous period of 43 years.
For seven of those years, I have been a Labour Member of Parliament.
For three of those years, I was a Shadow Minister. I was a Labour
councillor for twenty years and served twice as Leader of a Labour
council. Before this and throughout my period in office, I have been a
committed and loyal activist. This loyalty has extended to remaining in
the Party and defending its values even when these have been let down
by various leaders over the past four decades. My commitment has
never been in question and my loyalty has never wavered, whether
Labour has been in government or in opposition, or whether the left or
right wing of the Party has been in the ascendancy.

In 2010, I contested Derby North for the Labour Party and won against
the odds after a hard-fought campaign. In 2017, I secured the seat for
the Labour Party again standing on a platform of supporting Jeremy
Corbyn's vision to govern for the many, not the few. I was reported to
be the candidate whose values most closely aligned with Jeremy's
nationally and my campaign locally was perceived as a 'test case for
Corbynism'. In 2014, I was recognised as the most loyal Labour MP in
Parliament by the Parliamentary Internet, Communications and
Technology Forum. I am proud to represent my Party and fight for its
Leader, a man of honour whose leadership has already transformed our
political landscape and under whose premiership the principles we
stand for would be realised – taking millions out of poverty; addressing
our housing and homelessness crises; saving our NHS and schools from

stealth privatisation and a race to the bottom in standards; an ethical foreign policy and a transformation of the relationship between citizen and state.

Witch Hunt screening –
4ᵗʰ March 2019

1) Did you book a room in Parliament for 4th March 2019 to screen a film entitled 'Witch Hunt'?

Yes.

2) Please explain your understanding of the film.

'Witch Hunt' is the story of the black Jewish anti-racism trainer and activist Jackie Walker, who was suspended and subsequently expelled from the Labour Party as a result of a three-year organised campaign of pressure on the Party and its complaints system. The film shows that this campaign primarily targets Jewish Labour Party members and those in the Party deemed to be most closely aligned with Jeremy Corbyn. It is a tale that highlights the personal struggle and pain caused to ordinary Labour Party members as a result of this campaign. I had already seen the film and did not intend to attend the screening.

Jewish Labour Party members and organisations involved in making the film, (including but not limited to Jewish Voice for Labour [JVL]), have been systematically harassed by those leading the organised campaign of pressure on the Party, its complaints team and its Leader.

In 2018, on the fringes of the Labour Party Conference in Liverpool, JVL was threatened that the screening it had organised of an earlier biographical film about Jackie Walker's history of anti-racism would be bombed.[215] In undercover footage published by *Al Jazeera* in 2017, former Israeli Embassy operative and Jewish Labour Movement National Director Ella Rose said of Jackie Walker: *"I saw Jackie Walker on Saturday and thought: You know what? I could take her – she's like 5'2" and tiny".*[216]

In 2018, at a rally organised by the Board of Deputies of British Jews to campaign against Jeremy Corbyn's leadership of the Party, right-wing and far-right protesters associated with the Board of Deputies rally crossed over to a counter-protest where they harassed elderly Jewish women supporters of Jeremy, calling out "*kapo*" and claiming these Jewish women would be "*first into the ovens*" under a Labour government. One young Jewish man was reduced to tears after being told to "*go back to the ghetto*".[217] At this rally, Labour MPs unwittingly stood among far-right extremists who wore symbols associated with anti-Palestinian terrorism and the violent, racist Kahanist movement (formally banned in Israel and regarded as a terrorist organisation by Israel's allies). Some of those extremists wore t-shirts bearing the image of Menachem Begin – who masterminded the terrorist bombing of Jerusalem's King David Hotel in 1946 which killed 91 people – and later served two terms as Israeli Prime Minister.

On 4th September 2018, Jewish Labour Party members gathered in large numbers to protest outside Party headquarters against the adoption of the examples contained in the International Holocaust Remembrance Alliance (IHRA) definition of anti-Semitism by the Party – led by JVL. A small counter-demonstration in support of the Labour Party adopting the IHRA examples was almost exclusively attended by known far-right activists.

On the same day as this protest, I received a stream of abuse over a megaphone from Damon Lenszner outside the Party's headquarters while attempting to give media interviews outlining the position of the majority of Party members I have spoken to across the country towards the IHRA examples. Mr Lenszner repeatedly screamed "Labour fascist" and described me as "at the top table, eating the scum off Corbyn's plate". The incident was recorded on camera.[218] I note that Mr Lenszner and Jonathan Hoffman, who is former vice-chair of the Zionist Federation, were recently issued with warrants after they failed to appear at Westminster Magistrates' Court. Mr Lenszner was charged with assault by beating and Mr Hoffman with common assault and using threatening words and behaviour under Section Four of the Public Order Act.

In my view the Party has been institutionally absent in the defence of Jewish socialists while abuse against them is normalised by extremist groups.

The apparently targeted, organised campaign of malicious and vexatious complaints which disproportionately targets left-wing Jewish Party members addressed by the film is, in my experience deplored by the membership at large. This campaign has been supported by some in the PLP in good faith because they are unaware of the links between this campaign and far-right ideology. This is, in my view, due to a major gap in the Party's political education offering on the origins and nature of the war for Palestine and how that conflict affects contemporary politics, including in the UK.

The Party must address these problems in order to protect left-wing Jewish members and fight anti-Semitism. It is patronising and insulting to assume that pro-Israel groups speak for Jewish members or British Jews in general. Left-wing Jewish members tell me they regard this monopoly on opinion as anti-Semitic because it inaccurately and unfairly equates Jewish identity with support for a political ideology they regard as racist. The relationship between the organised campaign of harassment targeting our Jewish members and the far-right is also a national security issue – both in respect of domestic extremism and foreign interference in our democracy.

To better understand the international dimensions of the far-right's role and motivations and to contextualise the national security issues at stake, I encourage NEC members to read a recent article entitled 'Why the new nationalists love Israel' by the *Financial Times* columnist Gideon Rachman on the subject of Israel's cultivation of far-right alliances across Europe. Mr Rachman is by no means a man of the Left and writes from a perspective that is supportive of Israel, and yet he observes that:

'These days, Europe's far-right is far more hostile to Muslims than Jews, and that Islamophobia often translates into support for Israel.'[219]

3) Please explain why you booked a room in Parliament to screen this film.

'Witch Hunt' is an account of the systematic abuse, threats of violence and centralised, industrial-scale online harassment faced by Jewish supporters of Jeremy Corbyn's leadership. I was not scheduled to give a talk or to be present at the event but I believed it to be essential that the film ought to be shown in Parliament, in a secure environment for our internationalist socialist Jewish members, whereas outside Parliament they are routinely harassed by far-right street thugs and others, resulting in a bomb threat at Conference 2018 as mentioned above. I was merely a facilitator in respect of the prospective screening of the film.

An underlying argument of the film is that if those orchestrating the campaign against our members and the Party Leader cannot prevent Labour winning the next general election, they intend to ensure a Labour government cannot make any substantive changes to foreign or domestic security policy, thus neutralising the supposed 'threat' posed by Jeremy's leadership. In contrast, I perceive Jeremy's leadership to be the best prospect for millions of the most vulnerable in our society to reclaim their dignity after nine punishing years of Conservative rule.

As a Labour Party member of 43 years and a Labour MP supportive of Jeremy Corbyn's leadership, I believe it is essential that parliamentary colleagues, Party members and the public should understand the origins and nature of the campaign against the Party, and specifically against Jeremy's leadership. I see that this film is a valuable teaching resource about the ongoing campaign against Jeremy's leadership and the Party as a whole.

4) Do you have anything else you think the Party should know about this screening?

I was contacted by Jewish members of the Party to ask whether I would be able to host the screening in Parliament.

The film is an important learning resource for Labour Party members of all ranks. For more context on my decision to support the screening of this film in Parliament and so as to better acquaint themselves with the origins and nature of the campaign against allies of the Party Leader, NEC members should watch the film and can do so here: https://witchhuntfilm.org/.

Sheffield Momentum meeting –
23rd February 2019 – Item 1

5) Did you speak at a meeting of Sheffield Momentum on the 23rd February 2019?

Yes.

6) During this meeting did you say "The Party...is being demonised as a racist bigoted party...I think the Party's response has been partly responsible...we've backed off on too much, we've given too much ground, we've been too apologetic"? If so, please explain what you meant when you said this.

I used some of those words but they were not delivered as presented above.

The selective and highly misleading quote above is without context and appears to have been provided maliciously and vexatiously by a third party with the deliberate intention of my words being misconstrued. The NEC's investigation process should be neutral, beyond reproach and should not rely on politically motivated briefing campaigns by third parties motivated against the Party and its Leader.

As a serving MP or as a Party member, I reasonably expect the Party to conduct its own basic research regarding alleged misconduct before imposing a disciplinary sanction as serious as suspension, particularly when it is attached to accusations of anti-Semitism and the consequential reputational damage I have and continue to endure.

If the Party fails in this basic duty of clarifying and verifying allegations made by malicious and vexatious third parties before imposing suspension (as is the case here), I have justifiable reason to doubt the transparency, robustness and fairness of the disciplinary process, and question whether the actions taken against me have been in the interests of the Party and the public.

For the avoidance of doubt, and by way of accurate disclosure, a transcript of the relevant part of my speech in Sheffield is provided below.

"We are not a racist party, are we? We're not an anti-Semitic party. We are the Party that stood up to racism throughout our entire history. It was Labour, and Jeremy's mam, standing shoulder-to-shoulder with the Jewish community in Cable Street fighting Oswald Mosley's fascists. It was Labour that was the backbone of the Anti-Nazi League in the 1970s when we confronted the anti-Semites, the racists, the Islamophobes on the streets and we defeated those fascists, didn't we? And now we – Jeremy, me and others – are being accused of being bigots, of being anti-Semites. And it's almost as we're living within the pages of George Orwell's 1984. You know the Party that's done more to stand up to racism is now being demonised as a racist, bigoted party.

And I've got to say I think our Party's response has been partly responsible for that. Because in my opinion – I never have, I've got to say – we've backed off far too much, we've given too much ground, we've been too apologetic. What have we got to apologise for? For being an anti-racist party? And we've done more to actually address the scourge of anti-Semitism than any other political party. Any other political party. And yet we are being traduced. And grassroots members are being traduced. And I'm not going to stand up and tolerate that in any way shape or form and whenever I get the opportunity [inaudible] I will not allow these people to slag off decent, hard-working, socialist members of our Party. I'm just not going do it because it's an absolute bloody travesty what they're saying about Party members."

7) **During this meeting, did you claim to have sung 'Celebration' outside the office of Joan Ryan MP after**

she resigned from the Party. If so, please explain what you meant when you said this.

No. In a light-hearted interview with the *New Statesman*'s Kevin Maguire, I stated that I had sung 'Celebration' inside my office which was opposite Ms Ryan's office. She would not have heard me. I did not sing 'outside the office' of Ms Ryan. I cannot claim that I was disappointed when Ms Ryan left the Party and believe that those sentiments are shared by the overwhelming majority of Labour Party members.

Joan Ryan is no longer a Labour Party MP or a member of the Party. The majority of the active members of Enfield North CLP appear to be deeply grateful for this. She lost a no confidence vote called by members of her CLP – an extraordinary step for members to take – in September 2018.[220]

Her response was to describe members of her own CLP as "*Trots Stalinists Communists and assorted hard left*" (sic) on Twitter and to claim that she had no confidence in them.[221] Ms Ryan's conceited behaviour and disregard for members clearly brought the Party into disrepute under Rule 2.1.8 and undermined members' confidence in the Party's procedures, as well as damaging the standing of Parliament and MPs at a time when we needed to do more to connect with those we represent.

Ms Ryan's comments constituted a direct and public attack on Party members by a then Labour Party MP and were a clear breach of the Party's Code of Conduct: Social Media Policy. Disappointingly, no action was taken by the Party, which highlights the inconsistent and haphazard way in which the Party implements disciplinary action.

The vote of no confidence in Ms Ryan was preceded by a growing discontent among members in Enfield specifically relating to anti-black racism locally, and anti-Palestinian racism stemming from her chairmanship of Labour Friends of Israel.

The Skwawkbox reported extensively in 2018 on the controversial deselection of all black councillors in Enfield[222] – a borough where one in five residents is black – and what Labour Party members locally believed to be the cause.[223]

Local Labour Party members had also consistently expressed their outrage at findings by *Al Jazeera* relating to Ms Ryan in their 2017 documentary 'The Lobby'. As well as being caught on camera fabricating allegations of anti-Semitism against a Party member[224] [225] – an especially gross form of misconduct and abuse of power for an MP – Ms Ryan was also found discussing at Conference 2016 a £1m+ fund provided by the State of Israel with disgraced Israeli official Shai Masot,[226] who separately had plotted to "take down" a sitting Foreign Office minister on behalf of the State of Israel. Masot was immediately recalled to Israel to be disciplined once his government became aware of the documentary but Ms Ryan faced no censure from the Labour Party.

Following the broadcast of this documentary, Jeremy Corbyn wrote to the Prime Minister: *'This is clearly a national security issue. It is only [on the basis of an investigation] that Parliament and the public will be reassured that such activities will not be tolerated by your government.'*[227] Shadow Foreign Secretary Emily Thornberry called Masot's behaviour *'improper interference'* in our democracy.[228] Both Jeremy and Emily were absolutely right to demand a government inquiry into a subversion campaign targeted both at our Party and the Foreign Office. However, the Party did not discipline Ms Ryan.

Given that Ms Ryan defected to a pro-austerity, pro-war group of MPs organised not as a party but as a private company,[229] my comments in Sheffield – specifically that Ms Ryan *"left the Labour Party years ago, to be honest"* – have shown to be true.

It is a gross failing of the Party's disciplinary regime that Ms Ryan was allowed to leave the Party of her own volition even after her own CLP had deemed her unfit to represent the Party and she had been exposed as conspiring with a foreign official. Since leaving the Party, she has gone on to speak at the American-Israel Public Affairs Committee (AIPAC) Conference, which was boycotted by mainstream Democratic Party presidential candidates. I understand Ms Ryan was invited there to attack the Labour Party and its Leader and did so fulsomely.[230]   The Labour Party has not responded.

Below is the assessment of the new Vice Chair for Membership in Enfield North CLP of our Party's rise in popularity locally since

Ms Ryan defected,[231] and an interaction with a local resident who suggests they are now much more inclined to vote Labour after Ms Ryan's defection:[232] (Please see the Twitter link below for further on this).

8) Is there anything else you think the Party should know about this meeting?

No, but I think it is important for the Party to understand that in 2012 I had spoken in support of Ms Ryan at a local fundraising meeting. Over time, however, our views became irreparably disparate.

Gilad Atzmon Petition –
21st December 2018 – Items 2 and 3

9) Did you sign a petition entitled 'Hands Off Gilad Atzmon'? If so, please explain why you signed this petition.

I did not sign the petition and contacted Change.org to express my surprise after a Twitter user posted a screenshot of the petition page showing my name as a signatory. I have received confirmation from Change.org (Appendix 1) that my *'account does not show [your] signature in this petition.'*

I note that the picture in Item 2 purporting to be a screenshot of the petition page showing my signature was posted on 21 December 2018 to Twitter by the Conservative candidate for Odd Down Ward in Bath & North East Somerset Council, Alastair Thompson.[233] The picture he tweeted corresponds exactly with that shown in Item 2.

10) Please explain the reason for posting the tweet in Item 3.

See below.

11) Please explain your understanding of the Gilad Atzmon petition.

I was told by a Party member in Islington that the Town Hall had been lobbied to prevent Mr Atzmon, an accomplished and award-winning saxophonist, from playing there. I had never heard of Mr Atzmon and was unaware of his political, theological and cultural views. I was told in good faith by a trusted activist that Mr Atzmon was a former Israeli soldier who espoused pro-Palestinian views and was being censored on that basis. This appeared unjust and entirely plausible given the climate of fear encouraged by the growing number of malicious campaigns designed to shut down free speech on Palestine.

As a token of support, I tweeted a link to the petition which **automated** the wording of the tweet in Item 3. Within a couple of minutes, a deeply knowledgeable Party member and pro-Palestinian activist called me to ask if I was aware of all of Mr Atzmon's views. I was not and I confirmed the same. He told me that Mr Atzmon's ideas on 'Jewishness' racially characterise Jews; that Mr Atzmon had made Judeophobic remarks so extreme they could incite violence; and that the Palestinian solidarity movements of the UK had long dissociated from and denounced Mr Atzmon for these reasons. He also pointed me to articles that had been written by Palestinian advocates arguing that Mr Atzmon's views were dangerous.

On this advice, **I reacted promptly and deleted the tweet within twelve minutes of originally posting it**. As detailed above, I also contacted Change.org in respect of Item 2, a screenshot purporting to prove my signature of the petition. It has been confirmed that there is no 'indication that the screenshot was taken from the aforementioned petition' (Appendix 1).

I tweeted a full apology which said:

'APOLOGY

Earlier today I tweeted a petition about an Islington Council ban against The Blockheads performing with their chosen line-up. The Council has blocked jazz musician Gilad Atzmon from playing with the group. Since then I've learned that Atzmon, a former Israeli soldier, is not confined to the jazz world. I am told that in various blogs and in speeches he has adopted anti-Semitic language.

I wasn't aware of this until after I tweeted the petition. As soon as I was informed, I deleted the tweet. I've always condemned all forms of racism, including anti-Semitism, and strongly disassociate myself from Atzmon's anti-Semitic views.

I therefore apologise for tweeting this petition and any distress or offence it may have caused.'

12) Is there anything else you think the Party should know about this tweet?

The incident led me to consider even more carefully than before my chosen associates and the importance of taking sound and considered advice from well-informed sources. I take my responsibility to my constituents and to the Party very seriously as I have clearly demonstrated.

The fact that I did not sign the petition itself and that Change.org have confirmed this (Appendix 1) leads me to question how a screenshot (Item 2) could appear alleging that I had signed the petition.

It is known, for example, that those who are co-ordinating the malicious and vexatious campaign to malign Labour Party members and allies of Jeremy Corbyn have resorted to editing screenshots in their pursuit of their targets, as well as creating fake social media accounts posing as Labour Party members in order to post comments and content that would put these fake characters in breach of the Party's Rule 2.1.8 and Code of Conduct: Social Media Policy, with the objective of bringing negative media attention to the Party.

A particularly disturbing element of this campaign has been an effort to invent fake online personas that are Muslim who then post anti-Semitic content.[234] There are serious questions to be addressed about the Islamophobia driving this campaign.

Board of Deputies Tweet –

27ᵗʰ October 2018 – Item 4

13) Please explain the reason for posting the tweet in Item 4.

'Blow me down with a feather' is an expression of surprise. The article in the tweet (Item 4) refers to an anonymous community leader within the Board of Deputies of British Jews (BoD) accusing the BoD president Marie van der Zyl of using an "anti-Semitic trope".

Marie van der Zyl was attacked for her comments made during a Board meeting. The (Jewish) Chronicle reported:

Another senior communal source was highly critical of Mrs van der Zyl's latest remarks, telling the JC: "In what world do you use the words 'Jewish community' and 'power' in the same sentence?"

"The community has spent months highlighting antisemitic tropes and then the President of the Board of Deputies herself says Jews have power which they learn how to use.

"I don't know what's worse — that this was a spur of the moment comment or that it was actually planned?

"The Board is more worried about their positioning than getting the right answer."

14) Were you aware of the Pittsburgh synagogue shooting when you posted this tweet?

No.

15) Is there anything else you think the Party should know about this tweet?

My expression of surprise that the BoD president could be accused by another senior communal leader within the BoD of harbouring anti-Semitic ideas highlights the extent of confusion and disagreement in contemporary political discourse about what constitutes anti-Semitism.

As a social movement and a party with many Jewish members, the Labour Party has an important responsibility in this discourse so that anti-Semitism is defined in a way that protects Jews and does not allow for malicious and vexatious claims to distort the meaning of anti-Semitism, which would lead to British Jews becoming more vulnerable in the long-term.

Vanessa Beeley Tweet –
19th August 2018 – Item 5

16) Please explain the reason for posting the tweet in Item 5.

I was a guest speaker at the Beautiful Days Festival 2018. The Festival is organised by the rock band The Levellers. The Rebel Tent hosted political discussions on climate change, foreign policy, prospects for the Labour Party and LGBT rights. One of these discussions was entitled 'Syria – What is to be done?' and featured a discussion between the former British ambassador to Syria, Peter Ford, with the activist Peter Tatchell.

I had been a panellist on the previous panel, entitled 'A New Politics from the Left', discussing the Labour Party's rapid progress and its future under the leadership of Jeremy Corbyn. I decided to stay in the tent to hear the discussion on Syria and joined the audience.

During the discussion on Syria, Vanessa Beeley made an impressive contribution from the floor, speaking with authority and eloquence of her own substantial reporting experience in Syria. She also made the case against military intervention in the conflict. Her arguments that day most closely represented the Labour Party's position.

We met briefly towards the end of the event and I sent the tweet as a courtesy acknowledging that we had met. It is very common to use social media to 'tag' or acknowledge people who you meet in professional circles.

17) Please explain your understanding of who Vanessa Beeley is.

Vanessa Beeley is a reporter and researcher who writes for 21stcenturywire.com and has reported extensively from Syria. She was a finalist for the 2017 Martha Gellhorn Prize for Journalism.

18) Is there anything else you think the Party should know about this tweet?

No

Justice4Marc Manchester Meeting – 30ᵗʰ May 2018

19) Did you speak at a Justice4Marc meeting in Manchester on 30ᵗʰ May 2018?

Yes.

20) During the meeting, did you say "that's why certain dark forces are using their power, using their contacts in the media in order to undermine this project"? If so, what did you mean by this?

I have attached the full transcript of the speech for contextual purposes (Appendix 2). I urge NEC members to consult the transcript to fully understand the argument I was making in support of the Party and Jeremy's leadership.

Since late 2015, there has been an organised campaign of pressure targeting the Party, the Leader and the complaints system with the objective of ending Jeremy's leadership. This has taken many forms and emanated from a variety of sources.

Examples include (1) the *'improper interference'* in our democracy by a hostile foreign government referenced by Emily Thornberry in a letter to the Foreign Affairs Committee; (2) the Integrity Initiative – a taxpayer-funded information warfare campaign targeting the Labour Party, commissioned by the Foreign & Commonwealth Office (FCO), managed by British former military intelligence officials and outsourced to organisations such as Bellingcat, which has recently dedicated a full-time researcher to smearing Jeremy Corbyn and the Party;[235] and (3) Labour MPs opposed to Jeremy's leadership habitually bringing the Party into disrepute by briefing against the Leader's Office, leaking and co-ordinating personal attacks against Jeremy.

The first two are extremely serious national security matters and the latter is a disciplinary issue the Party should deal with.

I was deeply dismayed to be one of the few Labour MPs raising questions in Parliament over the Integrity Initiative's promotion of anti-Labour Party messages, which were paid for by the Foreign Office. Such a brazen, state-directed attack on our Party flies in the face of all democratic convention and seriously compromises the integrity of our press.

In respect of the PLP, Party members do not understand why, for example, when Dame Margaret Hodge called Jeremy a *"fucking anti-Semite and racist"* in the House of Commons in July 2018,[236] this was not met with any penalty or serious disciplinary sanction. There is also widespread dismay that Dame Margaret Hodge has recorded confidential conversations with the Party Leader and leaked material to the press – most recently to the *Sunday Times* last Sunday – and has faced no penalty or serious disciplinary sanction. Her behaviour has been described by the Party Leader as a *"total breach of trust"*.[237] I fully agree with his view.

Members have also described to me their lack of faith in the Party's disciplinary system given that Ian Austin MP faced no penalty or serious disciplinary sanction after he repeatedly screamed abuse at the Party's chair Ian Lavery MP and told the Leader to *"shut up and sit down"* in Parliament while Jeremy was at the despatch box giving a statement on the Chilcot Report and the UK's involvement in the invasion of Iraq. Mr Austin brought the Party into disrepute not only through his public abuse of the Leader but by disgracing a solemn moment during which the public would expect decorum to be maintained as the Party Leader commented on the thousands of tragic deaths during the invasion and the war that followed.

Both Mr Austin and Dame Margaret Hodge received warning letters, after which Mr Austin publicly and repeatedly refused to apologise for his conduct.

21) Who do you understand dark forces to refer to?

See above.

There are a range of 'forces' that seek to undermine the Party in co-ordination with tax-exiled newspaper owners who see the Labour Party's promise to govern for the many, not the few as a threat to their interests.

The consequences of this campaign to undermine Jeremy's leadership have been covered extensively in a paper by academics at the London School of Economics & Political Science entitled 'Journalistic Representations of Jeremy Corbyn in the British Press: From Watchdog to Attack Dog' (read here) and academics at Birkbeck, University of London working with the Media Reform Coalition of Goldsmiths, University of London. The 2016 paper produced by the Birkbeck and Media Reform Coalition team at the height of a supposed crisis in the Labour Party was entitled 'Should he stay or should he go? Television and Online news coverage of the Labour Party in crisis' (read here). The Media Reform Coalition and Aston University's Dr Tom Mills has written extensively on the subject of how distorted media portrayals of Jeremy Corbyn and his allies have affected the Party, such as in a 2017 article for *The Conversation* entitled 'Media bias against Jeremy Corbyn shows how politicised reporting has become'. The article summarises some of the academic and other research on this subject up until that point and can be read here.

Four years of incessantly hostile media coverage have laid the ground for serious and generalised violent radicalisation against the Left. We have already lost one colleague to a horrific act of violence. More recently, the growing size of far-right rallies and the normalisation of far-right rhetoric should be a serious cause of alarm for the Party and its members. This has not occurred in a vacuum.

A senior serving general threatened in the *Sunday Times* in September 2015 that the armed forces would take *"direct action"* to prevent a Corbyn government implementing defence reforms.[238] In the same piece, intelligence officials threatened they would withhold crucial intelligence from Jeremy and his Cabinet in the event of a Labour election victory. Then came the fabricated Czech spy stories. More recently, former MI6 chief Sir Richard Dearlove has in October last year[239] and February this year[240] briefed the *Sunday Times* and *Mail on Sunday* respectively against the Leader's Office. In September, sitting MI5 chief Andrew Parker did the same with the *Sunday Times*.[241]

This demonisation of Jeremy personally, his staff and MPs who support his policy agenda is organised, co-ordinated and emanates from **multiple** sources, within the UK and from various foreign governments. It has culminated in the shocking footage of 3rd Parachute Regiment troops using Jeremy's image as target practice in Afghanistan and *The Times* running a recent front page promoting the idea of a 'strongman' taking charge of our democracy.[242]

The Party must not be naïve about the scale of the challenge facing it. Party members and those deemed either politically or personally close to Jeremy are the primary targets of this campaign. The Party has weakened its position in facing down this challenge: firstly by failing to recognise the sources of this campaign and secondly by failing to implement a consistent standard in its disciplinary approach towards Party members and MPs.

This is particularly pertinent in light of findings in the LSE paper mentioned above, which states *'the British media has systematically attacked Jeremy Corbyn ever since he came to national prominence in the summer of 2015'*[243] and research by the Media Reform Coalition which states that '*BBC correspondents tended to ascribe militancy and aggression exclusively to Jeremy Corbyn and his supporters rather than Labour rebels, in spite of the fact that the leadership was, throughout this period (2016), largely on the defensive in responding to attacks and accusations by rebel MPs'*.[244]

Both reports are essential context for NEC members in assessing how my public comments have been persistently and maliciously misconstrued.

I note also that a 2016 YouGov poll found that 77 per cent of Labour members and 69 per cent of Labour voters believed that the mainstream media had been deliberately biasing coverage to portray Jeremy in a negative light.[245] Jeremy's allies and supporters in the Party, of which I am one, have obviously faced similar treatment and the complaints presented here should be viewed in light of that organised campaign as well as the campaign's effects on those who have been susceptible to its influence while acting in good faith.

22) During this meeting, did you say "Some people might find it a bit difficult to show solidarity with Marc, for fear of being...you know...implicated and criticised and demonised"? If so, what did you mean by this?

In the face of an orchestrated campaign of intimidation as described above, it is obviously difficult for Party members to defend those who have been unfairly targeted. Breaking those bonds of solidarity is a key objective of the campaign against our Party and its Leader. I have always been a strong advocate for solidarity within the Party and it remains a key focus of my work.

23) During this meeting, did you say "anti-Semitism is being weaponised and I think some people have weaponised it and I agree with that, that's pretty clear"? If so, what did you mean by this?

I did but it is of the utmost importance for the context to be understood and in particular the words that immediately preceded this line in my speech (paragraphs 58-59 of Appendix 2):

"So, it's good to see that Jennie Formby, who I've got the utmost confidence in, she's a great trade unionist, a great supporter of

Jeremy Corbyn, and she will be, I think, a wonderful, and is already proving to be a great general secretary of the party.

So she is bringing these new procedures in and there will be time limited processes; going to depoliticise the whole affair, which I think is also important because I know many people in the Jewish community have said to me, and it's been put at my door as if I've coined the phrase, and I haven't, it was people in the Jewish community who've said to me that anti-Semitism was being weaponised."

The idea of the 'weaponisation' of anti-Semitism is not one I originated. It has a long precedent among historians of Jewish political thought and among historians of Israel. I first encountered the phrase in a statement by the Jewish Socialist Group relating to the Labour Party dated 28 April 2016, which stated:

'Accusations of antisemitism are currently being weaponised to attack the Jeremy Corbyn-led Labour party with claims that Labour has a "problem" of antisemitism. This is despite Corbyn's longstanding record of actively opposing fascism and all forms of racism, and being a firm a supporter of the rights of refugees and of human rights globally.' [246]

I encourage all NEC members to read the statement, which expresses the sentiments of many left-wing Jewish Labour Party members whose voices are drowned out by the organised campaign to malign and marginalise them....

The words 'weaponise' and 'weaponisation' are used repeatedly by various sources in condemning allegations of anti-Semitism that are maliciously and vexatiously used by political opponents of Jeremy Corbyn and the Labour Party.[247]

I believe that bad faith accusations are being made against allies of the Party Leader in a bid to undermine his position. It is also the case that the Party's refusal to clearly identify the source of these politically motivated allegations as a malicious and co-ordinated campaign, which is part of the process of *'improper interference in our democratic politics by other states'* identified by Emily Thornberry in 2017, has allowed members to face trial by media.

The Party's encouragement and/or lack of action in relation to this trial by media, such as by breaching members' confidentiality and leaking details of disciplinary cases to hostile press, has led to increasing politicisation of anti-Semitism by opponents of the Party's mainstream and popular manifesto plan to transform our society.

Three examples are particularly instructive in demonstrating how the Party has facilitated and/or failed to take appropriate action in relation to malicious accusations and the politicisation of anti-Semitism. Firstly, that of Chuka Umunna, who said in a statement in October 2016 (reproduced in full on *Labour List*[248]) following the publication of the Home Affairs Select Committee report on anti-Semitism:

'Some have suggested that there is institutional anti-Semitism across the whole of the Labour Party – this is not a view I share, not least because I have not seen one incident of anti-Semitism in almost 20 years of activism within my local Labour Party in Lambeth. However, we would be putting our heads in the sand if we denied the existence of anti-Semitism amongst a minority in our wider Labour family – this is something our movement has a solemn duty to root out if we are to remain true to the principles we were founded to promote and protect.'

These are sentiments I wholeheartedly agree with. That Chuka Umunna MP was then able to accuse the Party of 'institutional anti-Semitism' less than two years later[249] as he made preparations to leave it is not exclusively an act of opportunism. It is also a failure of the Labour Party to articulate clearly and with authority the origins and cause of the outsized media attention on both genuine and unfounded claims of anti-Semitism among its members.

Recent assertions by Siobhain McDonagh MP on the Today programme (4 March 2019) that anti-capitalism is anti-Semitism[250] and Margaret Hodge MP on Channel 4 News (6 March 2019) that anti-Zionism is anti-Semitism[251] are stark evidence that accusations of anti-Semitism are being weaponised (i.e., used) to demonise internationalist socialism.

The Party's lack of a coherent understanding of what constitutes anti-Semitism and its refusal to call out such political instrumentalisation of anti-Semitism by opponents of the Leader puts Jews at risk. Ms McDonagh's and Dame Margaret Hodge's comments were met with scorn by the public – the risk, therefore, is that genuine anti-Semitism is not taken seriously enough. This would endanger British Jews and cannot be allowed to happen.

It is important for the Party to note that I have also repeatedly been the subject of weaponised allegations. The clearest example of this was the response by several organisations when I signed the Holocaust Educational Trust's Book of Commitment in Parliament, offering my sympathy and solidarity to Holocaust survivors. I wrote:

'Hatred and bigotry led to the unimaginable horrors of the Holocaust. We must never forget and always strive to build a better, peaceful and compassionate world through love and solidarity.'

There can be no possible interpretation of those words that could be reasonably construed as anti-Semitic. Such a suggestion would obviously be malicious and vexatious. Yet my contribution to the Book of Commitment and a photograph I tweeted of me signing the Book was met by the Jewish Leadership Council with "disgust" and described as a "smokescreen"; by the Board of Deputies with an accusation of "hypocrisy"; and by the Holocaust Educational Trust as "repulsive".[252] Given that I have been absolute and vigorous in condemning anti-Semitism, I have to question how anyone acting in good faith could arrive at such conclusions and whether concerns over anti-Semitism are indeed the motivation for such a response.

It is important to note also that the Holocaust Educational Trust took the photograph I tweeted of me signing the Book of Commitment and shared the photograph with me. The organisation did not, at the time I was signing the Book of Commitment, object to my doing so. This also leads me to ask which third party prevailed upon the organisation to issue an aggressive condemnation of me and with what intention. This malicious politicisation of solidarity with Holocaust survivors does not appear to have originated from the Holocaust Educational Trust but does fit a pattern of weaponisation of anti-Semitism for other political ends.

24) Is there anything else you think the Party should know about this event?

Marc Wadsworth is a black anti-racism campaigner with a long track record of educating others and fighting fascism on the frontline. He was an adviser to the family of Stephen Lawrence in the aftermath of Stephen's murder by racist thugs and was responsible for introducing the family to Nelson Mandela. I attended the event to support his reinstatement as a Labour Party member (offering solidarity) after he was, in my view the victim of a malicious, politically motivated and unfounded accusation of anti-Semitism.

It is important to note that in the same speech, I supported the progress the Party has been making both in attempting to clarify what constitutes anti-Semitism and in improving its disciplinary processes. I refer you to paragraphs 47-51 of Appendix 2 (the full transcript of my speech), which are also quoted below:

'And indeed, were the Chakrabarti recommendations implemented prior to Marc's absurd disciplinary hearing…well it wouldn't have even got to a hearing would it?

It would have been simply thrown out. So, it's good to see we are making progress because we should not tolerate, and nobody is suggesting that we should tolerate anti-Semitism or any form of bigotry. Of course we're not suggesting that. And for people to try and imply that that is what we are suggesting, well that's another calumny as well, and we must not let that stand either.'

Marc Wadsworth Hearing
25th April 2018

25) Did you attend a demonstration outside the NCC hearing of Marc Wadsworth on 25th April 2018? If so, please explain your reason for attending.

No. I accompanied Marc Wadsworth into the NCC hearing.

26) Is there anything else you think the Party should know about this demonstration?

I attended Marc Wadsworth's hearing to give evidence in person. Labour MPs Keith Vaz and Clive Lewis submitted written evidence.

Peterborough Momentum Meeting – 17th March 2018 – Item 6

27) Did you speak at a meeting of Peterborough Momentum on 17th March 2018?

Yes.

28) During this meeting, did you say "We've got these ridiculous suspensions and expulsions from the Party...in the most grotesque and unfair way"? If so, what did you mean by this?

Please refer to 20-23 above.

I note also the cases of Jean Fitzpatrick, Professor Moshé Machover and Glyn Secker, all of whom were placed under investigation in questionable and unfair circumstances. All were reinstated as members rapidly but confusion inside the Party about what constitutes anti-Semitism allowed them to be maliciously and vexatiously pursued, harming their reputations.

I note similarities between comments I made at the Peterborough meeting and page 18 of the Shami Chakrabarti Inquiry report:

'I find it regrettable, to say the least, that some subjects of recent suspension and disciplinary process, under the Party's disciplinary procedures, found out about their suspensions and investigations as a result of media reporting rather than notice from the Party itself. Staff or elected officials should never feel it necessary (even during a pre-election media frenzy) - to operate a presumption of suspension. If anything, the presumption should be against interim suspension. The question should be about the seriousness of any immediate damage that the person subject to investigation might do to the Party if allowed to continue as a member in the meantime.

Indeed, if the principle of proportionality had been properly applied in recent times, I query whether so many people would ever have been suspended at all, rather than simply given notice that they were being investigated in relation to a complaint that their conduct had brought or was bringing the Party into disrepute. '[253]

29) Is there anything else you think the Party should know about this meeting?

It was an upbeat meeting, characterised by camaraderie and optimism about the future of the Labour Party and the broader Left.

Guardian Article – 28th August 2017 – Item 7

30) Did you make the comments reported by The Guardian in Item 7?

Yes.

31) Please explain what you meant by saying "I'm not saying it never ever happens but it is a really dirty,

lowdown trick, particularly the antisemitism smears. Many people in the Jewish community are appalled by what they see as weaponisation of antisemitism for political ends".

Please see 20-23 above.

Jewish communal groups such as Jewish Voice for Labour, the Jewish Socialist Group, Jews for Justice for Palestinians, some Haredi communities as well as many individuals from across the British Jewish community have expressed deep concern about the **weaponisation** of anti-Semitism for political ends in relation to Jeremy Corbyn and the Labour Party (see footnote 32). A selection of letters to *The Guardian* on the subject from just one day in August 2015 elicits a wide range of arguments supporting precisely this point.[254] I could quote many more Jewish members who agree. From my own conversations around the country, I know that this is the majority view within our Party.

An excerpt from Naomi Wayne's August 2015 letter to *The Guardian* on behalf of Jews for Justice for Palestinians captures the essence of the sentiment I hear around the country:

'We take no position regarding the Labour Party leadership contest. However, we deduce that the use – and serious abuse – of accusations of antisemitism and the like is evidence of panic that someone who stands up for Palestinian rights might end up leading a major British political party.'

32) **Please explain what you meant by "I think for all the talk of Venezuela and antisemitism and the latest thing is sexism now, Jeremy's overwhelming landslide victories in the leadership elections and the general election mean people have stopped listening to the smears".**

Please see 20-23 above.

Jeremy Corbyn is obviously not sexist. At the time I made those comments, he was being portrayed as such by those who are responsible for the organised and targeted campaign against him and his supporters. My comments refer to this attempt to smear Jeremy.

TalkRadio – 20th September 2017

33) Were you interviewed by Julia Hartley-Brewer on TalkRadio on 20th September 2017?

Yes.

34) During the interview, did you say "I know some people have expressed anxiety and the abuse online is unacceptable, but that isn't from Labour Party members. There's no evidence as far as I'm aware [that] any of the abuse online is being perpetrated by them"? If so, please explain what you meant by this.

As part of the organised campaign of pressure on the Party, its complaints team and its Leader, political opponents of the Leader have attempted to suggest that the Leader has fostered a climate of intimidation and abuse in our Party. Nothing could be further from the truth. The political instrumentalisation of anti-Semitism by opponents of the Labour Party and its Leader have led to the mischaracterisation of far-right abuse as emanating from Labour Party members. This is not the case.

Recent online targeted harassment of Luciana Berger MP, for example, has been led by the far-right group National Action. In October 2014, the Hitler-obsessed Garron Helm targeted Ms Berger. After he was jailed, the BNP rallied to his cause.[255] In December 2016, the neo-Nazi Joshua Bonehill-Paine was sentenced to two years in prison for his support of Mr Helm's harassment.[256] More recently, the Islamophobe John Nimmo was jailed for abusing Ms Berger.[257] In 2018, another Hitler-obsessed far-right thug, Jack Coulson, was jailed on suspicion of a threat to kill her.[258]

Yet Party members and MPs are under the wrong impression that Ms Berger was being abused by Labour members. When members and Party officials are not availed of the facts, they are unable to make sound judgements. I urge NEC officials to pay close attention to the facts and the political motivations underlying the co-ordinated campaign against political allies of the Leader.

35) What is your response to the allegation that your conduct may be or have been in breach of this [Rule 2.1.8] rule?

I categorically reject that I have breached Rule 2.1.8 of the Party's Rulebook. I have never and would never show hostility and/or prejudice to **any** person on the grounds of a protected characteristic. I am a committed and long-standing member of the Labour Party and have consistently sought to uphold its values and that of the Leader. I have campaigned tirelessly in support of the Party and its ethos and have never sought to bring the Party into disrepute. I am disappointed by the unsubstantiated nature of the allegations categorised in the letter of 27 February 2019 that have been provided in a vacuum, without context and/or prior investigation by the Party. The letter makes reference to *'a large number of complaints'* and *'a pattern of behaviour'* without justification. I have not been privy to the *'large number of complaints'* and therefore cannot fairly provide comment. I do not believe that the examples provided show a *'pattern of behaviour'* that brings the Party into disrepute and I have been able to provide meaningful and balanced responses that clearly show that I have acted in good faith at all times. I have provided various examples of other Party members that have publicly brought the Party into disrepute and that have not been sanctioned. I question why there is such disparity in the implementation of disciplinary action within the Party and in light of the above, I challenge my suspension and the allegations against me.

36) The Party's Code of Conduct: Social Media Policy states that "treat all people with dignity and respect. This applies offline and online." Do you think the posts in this pack are consistent with this policy?

I have not breached the Party's Code of Conduct: Social Media Policy (the Policy) and I treat all people with dignity and respect.

I have cited at 12 above that the incident in respect of Mr Atzmon has led me to think even more carefully about my associations and to take advice from well-informed sources. I stand by this and will continue to adopt this approach in the future.

37) Looking back at the evidence supplied with this letter, do you regret saying, posting or sharing any of this content?

I publicly apologised in respect of the tweet concerning Mr Atzmon which demonstrates I heeded the advice I received and I took prompt action to remove the post immediately. I will continue to exercise care over my social media profile in the future.

38) Do you intend to post or share content of this nature again in the future?

I have never intended to post any content that would cause offence, show hostility to any person with a protected characteristic or bring the Party into disrepute. I would not intentionally do so in the future. I deplore any insinuation to the contrary.

Summary

I have been entirely honest and frank in my answers to the questions posed. I reiterate again that my suspension is onerous, unfounded and only seeks to ostracise me from a Party to whom I have been committed for 43 years. I am disappointed that the Party has not sought to thoroughly investigate the alleged complaints against me before taking action. I have highlighted that a number of the allegations are factually inaccurate or have been presented without context so as to misconstrue my words and/or intentions. The Party has shown, as demonstrated above, that it has failed to implement its own Rules and Code of Conduct consistently across its membership.

I request again that the suspension is lifted on the basis set out above. It is a draconian sanction that is having an adverse impact upon me, the Party and my vocation as an MP.

The Labour Party

Head Office

Southside, 105 Victoria Street, London SW1E 6QT

Labour Central, Kings Manor,

Newcastle Upon Tyne NE1 6PA

0345 092 2299 | labour.org.uk/contact

Mr Christopher Williamson

[address removed]

03 September 2019

Ref: A168248

Case No: CN-2904

Dear Mr Williamson,

Notice of investigation and administrative suspension from holding office or representing the Labour Party

Allegations that you may have been involved in a breach of Labour Party rules have been brought to the attention of national officers of the Party. These allegations include:

- Sending an email to a member of the public who had complained to you about your criticisms of Margaret Hodge MP that referred her to a video on YouTube. The video described Ms Hodge as 'cheapening and exploiting the memory of Jewish suffering'; 'trivialising the memory of the Holocaust'; and requesting that she 'get the hell out of the Labour Party'; among other offensive personal statements about her.

- Publicly legitimising or endorsing the misconduct of members or former members of the Party that the NEC has found, in its opinion, to be grossly detrimental or prejudicial to the Labour Party

- Undermining the Party's ability to campaign effectively against antisemitism by publicly characterising the disciplinary processes of the Party in relation to cases of alleged racism as politically motivated and / or not genuine.

It is important that these allegations are investigated and the NEC will be asked to authorise a full report to be drawn up with recommendations for disciplinary action if appropriate.

We note that you are currently suspended pending the determination of charges of alleged misconduct against you by the National Constitutional Committee. We write to give you formal notice that it has been determined that the powers given to the NEC under Chapter 6 Clause I.1.A of the Party's rules should be invoked, separately and in relation to the new allegations enclosed in this letter, to suspend you from office or representation of the Party*, pending the outcome of an internal Party investigation. Please note this administrative suspension shall continue until the Party has concluded this new investigation and determined its outcome, irrespective of what may be determined in relation to any previous allegations of misconduct for which you are suspended.

The administrative suspension means that you cannot attend any Party meetings including Annual Conference and you cannot be considered for selection as a candidate to represent the Labour Party at an election at any level**.

In view of the urgency to protect the Party's reputation in the present situation the General Secretary has determined to use powers delegated to her under Chapter 1 Clause VIII.5 of the rules to impose this suspension forthwith, subject to the approval of the next meeting of the NEC.

The General Secretary has appointed an Investigations Officer to arrange conduct of the Party's own investigation. Attached to this letter is the evidence pertinent to this case, along with a series of questions which require your response. Upon receipt of your answers, the Party will be able to conclude this matter as quickly as possible.

Please respond in writing to the London address at the top of this letter or by email to disputes@labour.org.uk quoting case number CN-2904 within 7 days of the date at the top of this letter.

[CW email address removed] is the email address that we will be corresponding with during the course of this investigation. If this email is incorrect please call 0345 092 2299 to update it.

The Labour Party's investigation process operates confidentially. That is vital to ensure fairness to you and the complainant, and to protect the rights of all concerned under the Data Protection Act 2018. We must therefore ask you to ensure that you keep all information and correspondence relating to this investigation private, and that do not share it with third parties or the media (including social media).

That includes any information you receive from the Party identifying the name of the person who has made a complaint about you, any witnesses, the allegations against you, and the names of Party staff dealing with the matter. If you fail to do so, the Party reserves the right to take action to protect confidentiality, and you may be liable to disciplinary action for breach of the Party's rules. The Party will not share information about the case publicly unless, as a result of a breach of confidentially, it becomes necessary to correct inaccurate reports. In that case we will only release the minimum information necessary to make the correction. **The Party may also disclose information in order to comply with its safeguarding obligations.**

The Party would like to make clear that there is support available to you while this matter is being investigated. There are a number of organisations available who can offer support for your wellbeing:

- You can contact your **GP** who can help you access support for your mental health and wellbeing.
- **The Samaritans** are available 24/7 – They offer a safe place for anyone to talk any time they like, in their own way – about whatever's getting to them. Telephone **116 123**.
- **Citizens Advice** - Provide free, confidential and impartial advice. Their goal is to help everyone find a way forward, whatever problem they face. People go to the Citizens Advice Bureau with all sorts of issues. They may have money, benefit, housing or employment problems. They may be facing a crisis, or just considering their options. **https://www.citizensadvice.org.uk/**
- If you have questions about the investigation process please contact the Disputes Team, whose details are included in this letter.
- If you have any questions regarding support available from the party please call the
Safeguarding Unit on **0207 783 1134** Mon – Fri 9:30 – 4:30.

It is hoped you will offer your full co-operation to the Party in resolving this matter.

Yours sincerely,

The Governance and Legal Unit

The Labour Party

c.c. East Midlands Labour Party, Derby North CLP

APPENDIX VII:
Chris Williamson's response to the new allegations

Response to questions raised in letter of 3 September 2019

1) Please see the evidence attached overleaf. The Party has reason to believe that these are your Facebook (Items 1 and 2), Twitter (Item 3), and email (Item 4) accounts. Can you confirm this is the case?

   Yes.

2) The Party further has reason to believe that you posted or shared the statements contained in Items 1 through 4 yourself. Can you confirm this is the case? If not, each individual piece of evidence is numbered so please specify which of the pieces of evidence you are disputing posting or sharing?

   Yes, I did post or share the statements contained in Items 1 through to 4.

3) Please explain your understanding of the statement "David Icke called [the ruling class] reptilian shapeshifting vampire aliens which is only a marginal exaggeration. Lol. Coldblooded, lying parasites who regard themselves as a different breed"?

   My understanding is that the Facebook user quoted was being hyperbolic or exaggerating for effect. This is clear from the context of the full statement.

4) **By commenting "We need to help people realise that Ken" are you indicating agreement or support for the statement above? If not, please explain what you meant by this.**

Mr Underwood said: "I'm not sure many people realise quite how radical is the mind-set of those born into the ruling class. It's exemplified imho in the huntin-shootin-fishin ethos (my emphasis)." I responded: "We need to help people realise that Ken (my emphasis)." Mr Underwood's comment was a reflection on the gap in empathy and compassion between the most privileged in our society and the working class. My brief reply was stating that the Labour Party needed to help the public understand the class critique that underlies its rhetoric and policies under Jeremy Corbyn's leadership. Your omission of the material and substantive part of his statement; its replacement with a throwaway hyperbole which he clearly indicated was a humorous aside; and your subsequent insinuation about my meaning, are unfortunate examples of the bad faith that has characterised my experience with the Governance and Legal Unit since my suspension.

Item 2

5) **Please explain your understanding of the statement "Jackie's suspension is absurd –and a travesty. Worse still, it belittles the efforts of those who genuinely want to tackle anti-Semitism rather than cynically use it as a political football"?**

Item 2 is a Facebook status authored by Red Labour; a socialist activist group founded by Ben Sellers. Mr Sellers worked on Jeremy Corbyn's campaign team as Jeremy contested the leadership. Since then, he has worked as a senior adviser to Shadow Business Secretary Laura Pidcock, a position he still holds. I shared the status to my Facebook friends. I supported Jackie Walker for reasons set out in pp.1-4 of my original submission in response to the first round of questions I received (16.04.19).

6) By sharing this statement are you indicating agreement or support?

Yes. I continue to support Jackie Walker, as I have set out above and in my previous statement. I would like to add that Jackie Walker's suspension was lifted eighteen days after I shared this post, which suggests that at the time the Panel members agreed with me and Red Labour.

Item 3

7) Please explain why you thought it was appropriate to defend the comments made by Scott Nelson even though you had been informed of the content of those comments?

I did not defend the comments made by Scott Nelson.

I was not aware of the full extent of them, and I then made the point that he had apologised for those comments. I believe we should have a space for people to apologise and make amends when they have done wrong. It is my understanding that Mr Nelson has now been re-admitted to the Labour Party

8) Do you think your comments were appropriate given that a member of your own staff had reportedly described Mr Nelson's conduct as "clearly... antisemitic".

I have never defended the comments that were made by Scott Nelson. Please see my response to question 7 above.

Item 4

9) Please explain your understanding of the Norman Finkelstein video in Item 4.

Professor Finkelstein is one of the pre-eminent academic authorities on the political legacy of the Holocaust. In his book The Holocaust Industry, he explains at length and with great clarity that instrumentalisation of the Holocaust for political ends by advocates of Israel has harmed the fight against genuine anti-Semitism video is an emotional plea by Professor Finkelstein, whose family were victims of Nazi war crimes, for the instrumentalisation of the Holocaust to cease in contemporary debates in the Labour Party, where this method is used to attack Jeremy Corbyn.

10) Please explain why you shared this video with a member of the public.

The email in Item 4 is an abusive message sent to me by a Conservative voter. Given the tenor of her communication, I did not see fit to engage her at length. Instead, I courteously pointed her to Professor Finkelstein's video because it most accurately surmises the views, I hear from Labour Party members across the country who are concerned with fairness in the disciplinary process –especially Jewish members who are angered by the instrumentalisation that Professor Finkelstein describes.

11) Were you aware that the video stated that the video described Ms Hodge as 'cheapening and exploiting the memory of Jewish suffering'; 'trivialising the memory of the Holocaust'; and requesting that she should 'get the hell out of the Labour Party'?

My understanding was that the video addressed the political instrumentalisation of the Holocaust, an issue which resides within

Professor Finkelstein's expertise and which closely adheres to the themes he addresses in his book The Holocaust Industry.

12) Do you think it is appropriate to attack personally other members of the Party as done in this video?

Professor Finkelstein makes a range of political arguments about an emotive subject. It is for his critics to engage with those arguments. Professor Finkelstein's message reminds us there is no monopoly on Jewish opinion.

13) Do you think it is detrimental to the Party to share these sorts of comments about another Labour MP to a member of the public?

I did not attack Margaret Hodge. However, robust disagreement between members and challenging or critiquing members' viewpoints is an important part of engaging in politics. I have been the subject of baseless personal attacks, as is clear from the message I received that is at item 4and the concerns I have previously raised with the

Party about the attacks to which I have been subject directly from other Labour MPs. As far as I am aware, the Labour Party has done nothing about those attacks. Moreover, many other MPs and members of the Labour Party have been the subject of personal attacks from MPs and Labour Party members, including Jeremy Corbyn, without any action being taken as a result.

Item 5

14) What is your knowledge of the membership status of the person interviewing you in this video?

I have no knowledge of the membership status of the person in that video.

15) Regarding the comments you made about freedom of speech in this video: do you believe that Labour Party members should be able to say things that are prejudicial and grossly detrimental to the Party without repercussion?

There are rightly limits to free speech in the law –particularly to prevent incitement and to protect minorities. What constitutes speech that is 'prejudicial and grossly detrimental to the Party' is a matter of political interpretation. Labour Party members across the country express concern to me that the Party's current interpretation of this is draconian and lacks credibility because this clause has so often been used to target socialist members. When the disciplinary process is no longer seen as even-handed, fair and credible, the Party's ability to campaign on a platform of building a fair society and a fair economy are harmed.

Item 6

16) What is your knowledge of the membership status of the person interviewing you in this video?

I have no knowledge of the membership status of the person in that video.

17) What is your understanding of Labour Against Zionist Islamophobic Racism (LAZIR)?

As far as I know, it is an activist group established this year.

18) Do you think that members of the Labour Party should "naturally be working with LAZIR"?

I have included a transcript of the conversation as Annex 1. I believe that Labour should work with a broad church of opinion in robust open debate, as set out above. LAZIR campaigns against the IHRA definition of antisemitism and for a one-state solution in Palestine. These are not the current, official positions of the Labour Party.

Nor, for many decades, were support for racial equalities legislation or gay marriage official Labour Party positions, and activists advocating for these landmark reforms were sometimes perceived by the Party as unpalatable extremists or a liability. Political parties, including ours, are often the most conservative actors in the political process and usually the last institutions to catch up with the changes taking place around them. I believe open discussion about complex issues is important, and that the Labour movement should promote debate as opposed to shutting it down. To do otherwise leads to "never ending guilt by association", which was the subject of the discussion here and appears to be the basis of many of the allegations made against me.

19) Do you agree with the interviewer that allegations of "transphobia" or "misogyny" are "all kinds of smears used to generate division in the movement"?

The insinuation in the question is undeserving of a further response. My record is well-known. Please see the answer to the question I was asked at Annex 2.

20) Please explain what you meant by "I don't think [trope] is a particularly helpful term"?

The interviewer asked me to define a 'trope'. I could not do so with clarity and made that point. My response, transcribed in Annex 3 below, is self-explanatory. I suggested that most people we are trying to communicate with and engage as members or voters would, rightly, also struggle to define the term and we should avoid jargon in our political communication.

Item 7

21) Why do you think it was appropriate to publicly defend and / or promote a person who has been expelled from the Labour Party for conduct that is prejudicial and grossly detrimental to the Party?

I have given a detailed response on pp.1-4 of my original submission concerning my views of Ms Walker's suspension and expulsion and I will not re-state them here.

Item 8

22) Did you tell the Independent "It's a tragedy that a tiny but noisy minority of party members want to trash the spirit of the Human Rights Act. It's one of Labour's greatest achievements. Maybe these malcontents have forgotten that Labour enshrined freedom of expression into British law nearly 21 years ago...If these mischief-makers are genuinely interest in winning the next election, they should pipe down and devote their energies to exposing the Tories and promoting a common-sense socialist programme"?

Yes.

23) Who did you intend the terms "malcontents" and "mischief-makers" to refer to?

This refers to members of the Parliamentary Labour Party who are opposed to Jeremy Corbyn's leadership and have attempted to prevent me from addressing public meetings around the country.

24) Please explain what you meant by "they should pipe down"?

I think my meaning is clear from the context. I meant that members of the Parliamentary Labour Party hostile to Jeremy's leadership should not prevent his supporters from communicating Labour's transformative socialist policy platform and should not prevent discussions on internal party democracy–the two issues I most commonly address in my public meetings around the country

Item 9

25) Were you aware at the time that you shared a platform with her that Melanie Melvin was auto–excluded from the party in 2017 and that she has previously claimed that the "Sarin gassing [in Syria] was filmed by the BBC at Pinewood on the orders of Mrs May and the Israeli lobby" and that Diane Abbott "could claim Jewish ancestry" so that "there'd be action" taken against people who bully her on Twitter?

I did not share a platform with Melanie Melvin, and I do not know who she is beyond whatever interaction I may have had with her on Twitter. It may be helpful to set out what happened at the meeting that took place in Brighton on 8 August 2019. The meeting was chaired by Greg Hadfield, and there were only two other invited speakers, which were myself and a woman who I had not met before but have since learned is called Asa Jansson. After the three of us had spoken, the Chair allowed anyone in the audience who wanted to speak some time with the microphone. Several people came up to speak, one of whom was Tony Greenstein. As far as I can recall, Ms Melvin did not speak at the event at all. If she did, she did not introduce herself. Following the event, I shared a video that Ms Melvin had recorded of a Jewish woman –whose parents are Auschwitz survivors –calling Jewish members of the audience up to the top of the small slope on Regency Square to express solidarity with me. I had no input in any of this. However, I was touched by the support of many Jewish members who came to stand with me. One of those members of the audience was Tony Greenstein.

As a politician, I interact in some way with hundreds and sometimes thousands of people every day at meetings and online. It is obviously unreasonable to expect an encyclopaedic knowledge of their biographies and membership status. Nor, in most instances, should such knowledge preclude interaction and debate.

26) Were you aware at the time that you shared a platform with him that Tony Greenstein was expelled from the Labour Party in 2018 for conduct that is prejudicial and / or grossly detrimental to the Party?

Whilst I was aware of Tony Greenstein's expulsion from the Labour Party, it is, as I have already outlined, incorrect to say that I shared a platform with him. I did not attend the event with any expectation that he would be there, or that he would speak at an open mic section of the event. Nevertheless, as I have stated, what constitutes prejudicial or grossly detrimental conduct is a matter for political interpretation, especially when the disciplinary procedure is consistently used as a political instrument.

27) Do you think it is appropriate for a Labour Party member who is an MP to share a platform with people who have been expelled or auto-excluded from the Labour Party?

Please refer to my responses above. The Labour Party under Jeremy Corbyn is a mass political movement with a broad base. When the disciplinary process is used disproportionately and unfairly, it becomes difficult for any reasonable observer to determine whether expulsion from the Labour Party is a reflection on the individual or on the Party's procedures. 'Auto-expulsion' is a draconian measure for a mass movement that attempts to draw its supporters from a diverse social base, and that attempts to expand rather than contract that base. In my view, it is a measure incompatible with the Labour Party's rhetoric and policies under Jeremy Corbyn

Further Questions

28) Rule 2.I.8 in the Party's rulebook states: "No member of the Party shall engage in conduct which in the opinion of the NEC is prejudicial, or in any act which in the opinion of the NEC is grossly detrimental to the Party. The NEC and NCC shall take account of any codes of conduct currently in force and shall regard any incident which in their view might reasonably be seen to demonstrate hostility or prejudice based on age; disability; gender reassignment or identity; marriage and civil partnership; pregnancy and maternity; race; religion or belief; sex; or sexual orientation as conduct prejudicial to the Party: these shall include but not be limited to incidents involving racism, antisemitism, Islamophobia or otherwise racist language, sentiments, stereotypes or actions, sexual harassment, bullying or any form of intimidation towards another person on the basis of a protected characteristic as determined by the NEC, wherever it occurs, as conduct prejudicial to the Party. The disclosure of confidential information relating to the Party or to any other member, unless the disclosure is duly authorised or made pursuant to a legal obligation, shall also be considered conduct prejudicial to the Party. "What is

your response to the allegation that your conduct may be or have been in breach of this rule?

I refer you to my submission of 16 April 2019 in which I made clear that I categorically reject breaching Rule 2.1.8 of the Party's Rulebook, and continue to do so in light of the questions put to me in your letter of 3 September 2019. I have never and would never show hostility and/or prejudice to any person on the grounds of a protected characteristic. I am a committed and long-standing member of the Labour Party and have consistently sought to uphold its values and that of the Leader. I have campaigned tirelessly in support of the Party and its ethos and have never sought to bring the Party into disrepute. I have been able to provide meaningful and balanced responses that clearly show that I have acted in good faith at all times in light of the above, I challenge my suspension and the allegations against me.

29) **The Party's Code of Conduct: Social Media Policy states that "treat all people with dignity and respect. This applies offline and online" do you think the posts in this pack are consistent with this policy?**

I have not breached the Party's Code of Conduct: Social Media Policy (the Policy) and I treat all people with dignity and respect. Had the Party had serious concerns about my understanding of this, they should have communicated that to me at the time of these perceived breaches of that code, some of which took place in 2016.

30) **Looking back at the evidence supplied with this letter, do you regret posting or sharing any of this content?**

I always treat people with dignity and respect.

31) **Do you intend to post or share content of this nature again in the future?**

I will continue defending the Labour Party and its values.

Annexes

Annex 1:

Interviewer: "I asked you in the meeting –we didn't get into too much detail about it, probably because we were quite rushed out there –but I asked you about the role of 'internal pressure groups', they might call them, such as JVL [Jewish Voice for Labour] and LAW [Labour Against the Witchhunt]. And the way that there seems to be never-ending guilt–by–association there, and the guilt–by–association leading to internal splits between people that should naturally be working together. And I gave you three examples: the JVL grouping, the LAW grouping –best represented by, perhaps, Tony Greenstein –and the new LAZIR grouping, led by someone called Peter Gregson, as far as I can tell. "Do you think that it's important that we scrutinise these claims and force these groups back together? Because, essentially, the division that's occurring between them is actually leading to a huge amount of resentment in the movement and division there. I mean, do you think we can do more work in that regard?"

Chris Williamson: "Well, I think it's important to try and work in unity, if and when we can. I mean, obviously, in certain circumstances there's going to be differences of opinion, there's going to be potential splits, and I think having a debate is a healthy thing. You can have healthy disagreements, and that's the nature of democracy. "But I think it is incumbent upon us, really, to try and work together. This is one of the points I was making in a different context to the Parliamentary Labour Party [meeting] a few weeks –or months, now it is –ago, where I was making the case that: 'Look, we're all Labour Party MPs, we all joined the Party – I would like to think –and stood for Parliament to try and promote social justice, an ethical foreign policy, and so on. And, yeah, we're going to have differences of opinion but let's try and find ways of working together'. "So, it's not always going to be possible, and we have to be realistic about that. But I think, wherever we can, all of us, it's incumbent upon us, to do our best to try and work together because that old labour movement maxim about 'Unity is Strength' is absolutely apposite, really. And whenever we are falling out with each other, we're letting, essentially, the establishment, the powers that be, those that really do wield power in the country –we're letting them off the hook.

Annex 2:

Interviewer: "Obviously, there's been a lot of debate. And I'm keen to push this further than just the big, public issue of antisemitism. I'm keen to push it into real realms and territory of the deal with, say, transphobia and misogyny as well. Because these are all kinds of smears that are used to generate division in the movement. And I don't know if it's deliberate or accidental or what it is. But what do you think the role of definitions are in this, and how important do you think they are?"

Chris Williamson: "Well, I mean, I think for some people they are important. But, for me, I would just refer back to, I think, a comment that Jeremy [Corbyn] was making the other day, talking about –I don't think he was talking specifically about the point that you've raised –but he was making the distinction between 'tolerance' and 'respect'. And he said it's not just about tolerating different people, backgrounds, faiths, whatever –it's about respecting people. And I think if we can embrace that notion of respect, I think that would take us a long way down the road of moving the movement on and avoiding some of these unseemly fall-outs that we've seen, which has scarred the movement over the last two years."

Interviewer: "So, I mean, would it be correct to characterise you as somebody who thinks that definitions aren't really that substantially important?"

Chris Williamson: [Sighs audibly] "I mean, I don't know whether I've thought about it that deeply. To be honest with you, my view is that we should respect people, we shouldn't judge people, and I think if you can have a kind of non-judgemental attitude and you can respect people, then I think that will carry you a long way in terms of avoiding some of the difficulties that we've found ourselves in over the last few years or so."

Interviewer: "Well, non–judgemental is a little bit of a step back from what the movement has to do, isn't it? Doesn't the movement, at some point, have to say, 'This person's crossed a line' in some cases

Chris Williamson:

"Well, maybe, yeah, true. As I say, there will be certain circumstances. But, I mean, people who join the movement, you'd generally like to think they are like-minded people. They join because they want to fight for social justice, they want to bring about an ethical foreign policy on the international stage.

"But, yes, sometimes people potentially do step over the line; that is why you have rules in the Party to deal with that. But they should be used sparingly, in my view, and not be the first port of call to suggest that people be expelled or whatever. Because sometimes people articulate in certain ways that it's more through ignorance, really, than malice. "And I think this notion of trying to understand and then trying to work with people –and to have a collective, supportive approach, rather than judging people and calling people out in that very overt way sometimes. Particularly with social media these days, there's this sense of quick-to-judge and dogpile and demonise people when they may have made a foolish comment –and it's fine to call them out for that –but work with people, try and help people to grow! "I remember speaking to a young person, who's very active in the Labour Party now, but they were saying – coming from a working-class background –and they were saying, initially, when they first started taking an interest in things, they were initially attracted by the kind of far-right rhetoric. And it was only through talking to others, and there was a local Labour councillor who got involved with the local boxing club where he was a member and started some of the political discussions and raising consciousness that he realised the error of his ways. But if you were to just demonise that individual, we may have lost him forever. And he's a great man – I wouldn't name the guy – but he's a hugely important figure, in my opinion, in his own constituency and has made a massive contribution. And there'll be thousands of people, millions of people potentially, like that out there. We need to be building this movement in all its diversity and bringing people in, rather than trying to keep people out.

Annex 3

"I think there are a range of probable definitions [for a "trope"]; I don't want to necessarily hazard my own. I know it's a term that's used. I don't think it's a particularly helpful term, to be honest with you. And I think if you spoke to a lot of people throughout the country –working class, middle class, you name it –if you speak to a range of different people, I think a lot of people would be not quite sure what that is, either. And so, I think it's really important that we're clear with our language and we don't use jargony term.

APPENDIX VIII:
Last Word

It is perhaps pertinent that, as the author of a book dealing with issues of anti-Semitism, I should provide my opinions on the wider Israeli/Palestinian conflict. These are my views alone; I am unsure how representative they are of wider 'left' political thinking.

My interest in this debated land predates the more recent political wranglings described in these pages. In the summer of 1991, as a 19-year-old bored with the factory work I was doing, I read somewhere about the opportunity for young people to volunteer to work on a kibbutz. That was how I found myself in a small office off Cheetham Hill, the heart of Manchester's Jewish community, signing myself up as a kibbutznik. It was remarkably straightforward and, perhaps best of all for me at that time, was absolutely free. Only a few weeks passed before I was boarding a plane at Manchester Airport bound for Tel Aviv.

The memories of the weeks that followed are still vivid: arriving in the darkness and waking up to a view of the Judean desert and mountains made familiar from the Bible stories of my childhood; rising before dawn to head to work on the date plantations; the incredible Levantine food - falafel, tabbouleh, dates, wonderful tomatoes and other vegetables that exploded with colour and taste; relaxing with other British volunteers around the swimming pool - scorpions and snakes basking on the hot poolside tiles.

As an idealistic, young socialist, there were many aspects to kibbutz life that appealed - the communality, for example. We worked together, ate together, lived together; a tight-knit, small community striving to make the desert bloom.

Now, the reader with an awareness of the broader Israel/Palestine context might, at this point, have some questions they want to ask the younger me. Questions like whose land was it anyway, perhaps? And, in fairness, the 19-year-old me was not blind to this. In truth, it would have been hard to be totally unaware, for I had been sent to work on kibbutz Niran.[259]

Surrounded by barbed wire, deep in the occupied West Bank, there was an unmistakable sense that we were part of an occupying force. The land I went to work on six days a week had been confiscated from the nearby Palestinian village, which I could see sweltering in the valley beneath us, hunkered under the relentless sun. To enter or leave the kibbutz, we needed to go through a guarded post, and regular army patrols increased our security. I remember how, early one morning, a klaxon sounded, and we were hurriedly told that there had been some kind of an attack on the gate and that we were to stay in our rooms. I never learnt the whole truth around this incident, but we were kept on site the next day, not permitted to leave for work as we usually would be.

The longer I spent there, the more the disturbing aspects of the relationships between Israelis and Palestinians became apparent. I should say that I liked the young Israelis who worked alongside me. They were friendly and honest, hardworking with a streak of idealism I hadn't encountered at home; a sense of being pioneers, of taking responsibility and forming their own lives.

One day, at work in the date plantation, I heard the gentle tinkling of bells getting closer - then goats appeared, chewing contentedly at anything they could find. An old man approached with his herd, two young boys helping him shepherd the flock. The young Israeli man who oversaw us volunteers seemed very familiar with them and, in what appeared to be fluent Arabic, beckoned them over to the shade of the trees. He explained that these were Bedouin, whom he liked - nomadic people who wandered where they pleased. We sat in the shade while the old Bedouin man made some strong, hot coffee over a fire of sticks and we ate some of the dates we had picked.

There were *other* Arabs that my Israeli friend didn't like, namely the Palestinians whose land this originally was. One night, after a few beers, he produced some photos from his military service which showed him standing triumphantly over a range of cowed and clearly terrified Palestinian prisoners. I remember an image of a dead Palestinian. These pictures would immediately be recognisable today as similar to the infamous photos of American soldiers at the Abu Ghraib prison. I wasn't so friendly with him from that day on.

Unfortunately, this young army veteran wasn't alone with such sentiments and, after some weeks had elapsed and we had gained the locals' trust, this reality became steadily more obvious. The term 'dogs', in reference to Palestinians, graced drunken conversations at the disco.

I eventually left the kibbutz and spent the weeks that followed travelling. It was a wonderful experience for a young man. I walked to an Armenian monastery high up a donkey path that clung miraculously to the perpendicular cliffs. Inside its incense-scented walls, a priest pointed out the English translation of the text from the ancient bible that stood open on the lectern, repeatedly highlighting the scripture and then a cave across an airy chasm that separated the opposing cliff. The text in question related to the episode where Jesus faced temptation by the devil.

I walked the walls of the ancient fort of Masada where, long ago, Jews who are still remembered as folk heroes had defied the might of the Roman Empire. I wandered the old streets of Jerusalem, mesmerised by the call of the muezzin over the age-old city, the rocking faithful at the Wailing Wall and the dark, crowded, pungent streets. Then, north I strolled to the Sea of Galilee - the ancient sea walls of Acre - before, eventually, leaving by ferry from Haifa bound for Greece.

I will never forget my time there. My experiences helped to form a lifelong interest in the area. From that point on, whenever the area was to hit the headlines, I pored over the accompanying newspaper reports closely; the places I read about more *real* because I had walked their streets. I started to read widely about Israel and its near-neighbours. Robert Fisk was then, and remains, my favourite author on the region. And slowly, the problems I had witnessed during my short time there coalesced into a formed, political position.

Bluntly put, I think it is undeniable that the Palestinians are the victims of an enormous historical injustice. Although one might view with sympathy those who - at that time - saw the creation of a Jewish state (of Israel) as a historical necessity, it should now be conceded that it was founded with a crime at its core, namely the Jewish takeover of Palestine. The Zionist dream seems, demonstrably, to have failed - its continuing survival built on the premise of keeping millions under military occupation. Whatever its achievements (and there are many, not least in the fields of culture and science), it is clear to me that 'there is something rotten in the state of Denmark'.

Perhaps it would always have turned out like this - a new nation inheriting a land marked by the blood shadow of those whose home it had been; a heart of darkness on the Mediterranean sea. To many right-thinking people though, much of the modern state of Israel now seems abhorrent. Its militarism. Its open and unapologetic ethnonationalism. The weird interweaving of a several-thousand-year-old narrative into an idea of divine right. That so many in Israel and elsewhere - notably amongst the evangelical community in the USA - believe that the lands 'belong' to the Jews by biblical decree, I find deeply disturbing.

Tragically, both sides - the Palestinians and the Jews themselves - are the victims here. The Palestinians, trapped as they are in the impoverished 'prisons' of the West Bank and Gaza, are the biggest losers, of course. But the Israelis also feel under siege and under attack. It is no wonder that so many of them have become embittered and sour, hiding behind their walls and nuclear weapons. It is, ultimately, a matter of great shame.

That the two-state solution has failed seems obvious at this juncture. The viability of a separate Palestinian state seems practically impossible anyway, given the size and extent of the Jewish settlements.

So, what to do? Do I think the Jews should be 'driven into the sea'?[260] No, of course not. I think, just as in post-apartheid South Africa, something along the lines of an Israeli-Palestinian 'truth and reconciliation movement' should occur,[261] with both sides able to voice the hurts and wrongs they believe to have been committed. And then, when all parts of the community have been allowed their say, an attempt should be made to move on. Surely this is better than the cyclical rut of violence that is a depressingly permanent feature of the region?

And what would 'moving on' look like? For me, I believe there is only one viable remedy: a one-state solution and new democratic land of Israel/Palestine. I realise this would not be easy and would be fraught with danger. But this, a homeland for everyone, where citizenship would be on an 'equal basis for all', would offer hope for a feasible, long-term peace. That the current situation, a small state divided by walls and arms into mutually competing enemies, is doomed to failure, would seem obvious to a child, never mind a rational politician.

APPENDIX IX:
Timeline

1760 – The founding of the Jewish Board of Deputies (BoD)

1879 – Wilhelm Marr wrote 'Der Weg zum Siege des Germanenthums uber das Juendthum' (The Way to Victory of Germanicism over Judaism). First usage of the term 'anti-Semitism'

1917 – The Balfour Declaration: a public declaration of support by the British Government for a 'national home for the Jewish people' to be established in Palestine

1937 – Peel Commission: this recommended, for the first time, the partition of the land between a Jewish state and a Palestinian one

1948 – Founding of state of Israel

1976 – Chris Williamson joins the Labour Party

1981 – Gilad Atzmon takes part, as an Israeli soldier, in the war against Lebanon

1991 – Chris Williamson becomes a Labour councillor

2002 – Chris Williamson becomes leader of Derby City Council for the first time

8th February 2005 – Ken Livingstone becomes involved in a verbal fracas with journalist Oliver Finegold. Allegations of anti-Semitism were to dog him from this point on

3rd March 2009 – Corbyn appears at a 'Stop the War' coalition meeting where he voices the word "friends" in connection with Hamas. This quote, widely taken out of context, is now extensively used as evidence of his supposed anti-Semitism

January 2010 – Luciana Berger is 'parachuted' into the safe Labour seat of Liverpool Wavertree. Wins the forthcoming general election

6th May 2010 – Chris Williamson wins the parliamentary seat of Derby North. Becomes a Labour MP

13th October 2014 – a non-binding Labour backbench motion to recognise the Palestinian state wins the support of MPs in the Commons

7th May 2015 – Berger retains her seat in the general election. Williamson loses his in a closely fought battle. Corbyn is to call this the "worst" result of the night

18th July 2015 – In a first for the mainstream media, *Daily Telegraph* journalist Andrew Gilligan links Corbyn's 'friends' comment from 2009 to anti-Semitism

28th April 2016 – Livingstone is interviewed by Vanessa Feltz on BBC Radio London. Comments made during this, referring to Hitler's support for Zionism, cause another furore with allegations of anti-Semitism surfacing once more

27th June 2016 – As part of a long, orchestrated coup against the Corbyn leadership, organised by Labour MPs Hilary Benn and Margaret Hodge, Luciana Berger resigns her position as Shadow Minister for Mental Health. The coup fails

16th October 2016 – the House of Commons Home Affairs Committee publish its report into anti-Semitism. Its findings, subsequently and conveniently neglected, find the Labour

Party no more culpable of anti-Semitism than any other political party

8th June 2017 – Williamson wins back the Derby North seat in the general election. The local campaigning is notable for the widespread popular support Williamson mobilises

19th July 2017 – The Jewish Voice for Labour (JVL) is founded. The new organisation arises out of fears that the Jewish community was, unwittingly, being co-opted by the political right as part of their machinations against Corbyn and the left. It continues to reject accusations that the Labour Party is institutionally anti-Semitic

12th September 2017 – the Institute for Jewish Policy Research (JPR) publishes *Antisemitism in Contemporary Great Britain: A Study of Attitudes Towards Jews and Israel* which finds that: "Levels of antisemitism among those on the left-wing of the political spectrum, including the far-left, are indistinguishable from those found in the general population"

21st May 2018 – Tired of continual, baseless attacks, and the endless political distractions they are causing, Ken Livingstone resigns from the Labour Party

5th July 2018 – Labour's National Executive Committee (NEC) adopts the 38-word acting definition of the IHRA, but omits some of the more controversial examples it provides. This provokes anger amongst the Labour right and the wider Zionist movement

17th July 2018 – Margaret Hodge calls Jeremy Corbyn a "fucking anti-Semite" and a "racist" in frustration at the NEC refusing to adopt the IHRA definition in full

26TH July 2018 – In an unprecedented joint editorial, Jewish newspapers *The Jewish Chronicle*, *Jewish News* and *Jewish*

Telegraph describe a potential Corbyn-led Labour government as an 'existential threat' to the Jewish community

28th August 2018 – Jonathan Sacks gives an interview to the *New Statesman* in which he openly describes Corbyn as an 'anti-Semite'

4th September 2018 – after weeks of pressure, the NEC rolls over and adopts the IHRA antisemitism definition in full

21st December 2018 – Williamson faces allegations of anti-Semitism after tweeting in support of Gilad Atzmon who Islington Council banned from playing a concert with his band, The Blockheads

3rd February 2019 – WitchHunt, the film, is released. It covers the story of Labour activist Jackie Walker being expelled from the party on alleged ground of anti-Semitism

18th February 2019 – To the surprise of very few, seven Labour MPs - including Luciana Berger - quit the party to join a new group. (This short-lived political venture eventually becomes Change UK and meets with universal disinterest from the electorate.)

20th February 2019 – *The Guardian* publishes a letter signed by over 200 prominent members of the British Jewish community who voice their support for Corbyn as "a crucial ally" and the need for "freedom of expression" over Israel as with other countries

23rd February 2019 – Williamson attends a Sheffield Momentum meeting. An excerpt of his speech is leaked to the media (in which Williamson voices his opinion that the Labour Party needs to be more combative in dismissing false claims of anti-Semitism). This leads to him being embroiled in further allegations of anti-Semitism

27th February 2019 – Jonathan Freedland writes an article for *The Guardian* demanding that Williamson is suspended from the Labour Party. Williamson is duly suspended from the party later that day

27TH June 2019 – Williamson is readmitted to the party provoking howls of outrage

28th June 2019 - The Labour Party, caving in almost immediately to the pressure, re-suspends Williamson

9th July 2019 – *The Guardian* briefly publishes a letter of support for Williamson signed by over 100 prominent Jewish people, then soon deletes the letter from its website on the grounds that a small minority of the people listed as signatories were not who they claimed to be

10th July 2019 – a BBC Panorama documentary, 'Is Labour Anti-Semitic?' screens. It includes a range of testimonies from witnesses who are later found to be involved in efforts to undermine Corbyn and the left from within the party

10th October 2019 – Judge Pepperall gives his verdict on the 'Labour vs. Williamson' case. Williamson is awarded all his legal fees as the judge finds that the party acted improperly in their re-suspension of Williamson. Unfortunately, he also decides that the current, new allegations should be allowed to be investigated, thus ruling out Williamson being able to stand as a Labour MP in the upcoming election

6th November 2019 – Williamson resigns from the Labour Party and announces his decision to stand as an independent in the general election

12 December 2019 – Labour lose Derby North to the Conservatives

4th April 2020 – Keir Starmer is elected as the new head of the Labour Party

12th April 2020 – An internal Labour report regarding anti-Semitism within the party is leaked to the media. In pages of explosive testimony it relays how key figures inside the party worked to undermine the left and details their abusive behaviour. In the days that follow, Starmer announces that Labour will commission an "urgent, independent investigation" (the Forde inquiry) into this report and the circumstances around the leak

25th June 2020 – *The Independent* publishes an article on actress Maxine Peake where, buried within it, she makes the connection between the death of George Floyd, US policing, and Israeli training. Rebecca Long-Bailey, who retweets this newspaper article from her constituent, is sacked from her front bench role by the leadership

29th October 2020 – The long-awaited investigation report by the EHRC is published and gains vast media coverage. Interestingly, Williamson, after raising the prospect of a legal challenge, is not named

29th October 2020 – Corbyn releases his statement in response to the EHRC report. In it he says "The scale of the problem was also dramatically overstated for political reasons by our opponents inside and outside the party, as well as by much of the media." Almost immediately Starmer releases his own statement saying that those who believed the issue of anti-Semitism in the party had been "exaggerated" or was a "factional attack" are also "part of the problem and... should be nowhere near the Labour Party". After refusing to retract his statement or make a further apology, Corbyn is suspended from the party

29th November 2020 – In an interesting intervention into a process which is supposed to be independent, deputy Labour leader Angela Rayner announces that she will suspend "thousands and thousands" of members unless they "get real" about anti-Semitism in the party

7th May 2021 – Labour lose the seat of Hartlepool (in a by-election) for the first time in 62 years: the Tory candidate Jill Mortimer (51.9%) battering the Labour candidate Paul Williams (28.7%) in a contest which shows Labour consistently behind in the polls. The success of the Labour Party strategy in combatting the damaging false claims of anti-Semitism remains hard to see, as predicted by Williamson in his Momentum speech two years prior

4th June 2021 – Labour members still await the results of the "urgent" Forde inquiry set up more than a year ago

2nd July 2021 – Labour manage to crawl over the line by 323 votes in winning the Batley and Spen by-election much to the relief of Keir Starmer. Oddly described by some as "resounding" (Kim Leadbeater/Labour 35.3%, Ryan Stephenson/Tory 34.4%, George Galloway/Workers Party 21.9%), the result does little to instil faith in the party as a whole

Jeremy Corbyn remains suspended from the Labour Party.

Chris Williamson remains very active in left wing political circles – particularly the new 'Resist' movement.

Endnotes

Preface

1 *Oxford Paperback Dictionary & Thesaurus,* Oxford, 2009, p.37
2 https://www.jewishvirtuallibrary.org/anti-semitism-or-antisemitism
3 Dr Scott Ury of Tel Aviv University cited in Jonathan Judaken,
'Introduction – AHR Roundtable: Rethinking Anti-Semitism'
American Historical Review (2018) 123 (4) p.1132
<https://doi.org/10.1093/ahr/rhy024> accessed 29 September 2020.
4 p.1126
5 p.1127
6 The observant reader will note that the unhyphenated 'antisemitism'
is evident on the pages that follow. This, admittedly unsatisfactory
state of affairs, arises from the author respecting others' preferred
spelling in references and quotes
7 p.1132
8 *Oxford Paperback Dictionary & Thesaurus,* Oxford, 2009, p.1076
9 Benny Morris, *Righteous Victims: A History of the Zionist-Arab
Conflict, 1881-1998* (Vintage Books 2001), p.138.
10 Nur Masalha, *Expulsion of the Palestinians: The Concept of
"Transfer" in Zionist Political Though, 1882-1948* (Institute for
Palestine Studies 1992), p.107.
11 Stanley Porter et al (eds), *Faith in the Millennium* (Sheffield
Academic Press 2001), p.79.
12 Norman Rose, *'A Senseless, Squalid War': Voices from Palestine;
1890s to 1948* (Pimlico 2010), p.71.

Introduction

13 https://www.theguardian.com/commentisfree/2019/jun/27/labour-
chris-williamson-mp-antisemitism
14 https://www.bbc.co.uk/news/uk-politics-48790803
15 https://www.bod.org.uk/chris-williamson-readmission-is-an-utter-
disgrace/
16 https://www.theguardian.com/politics/2019/jun/27/chris-
williamson-labour-mp-suspension-lifted-antisemitism-anger-jewish-
members

Chapter 1 – The Manufactured anti-Semitism Crisis

17 https://www.theguardian.com/books/2020/sep/19/owen-jones-a-lot-of-people-in-the-parliamentary-labour-party-are-horrible
18 This article is of interest on that https://www.latimes.com/archives/la-xpm-1992-11-22-tm-2025-story.html. Also please note that I am all too aware of how this 'socialist' future that many of the kibbutzniks worked for was only for the Jew, with the Palestinians, often only a stone's throw away, excluded from that vision. This is the fatal flaw at the heart of the Israeli story.
19 https://www.theguardian.com/commentisfree/2019/nov/26/british-jews-corbyn-emigrate
20 https://www.thejc.com/news/uk/labour-was-catastrophic-on-israel-says-shadow-cabinet-member-michael-dugher-1.66832
21 https://antisemitism.org/politics/labour/jeremy-corbyn/
22 https://www.belfasttelegraph.co.uk/news/northern-ireland/tony-blair-thanks-martin-mcguinness-for-his-service-and-leadership-35382467.html
23 https://www.thejc.com/news/uk/jeremy-corbyn-tells-commons-committee-ken-livingstone-s-hitler-comment-was-wholly-unacceptable-1.60111
24 https://www.telegraph.co.uk/news/politics/labour/11749043/Andrew-Gilligan-Jeremy-Corbyn-friend-to-Hamas-Iran-and-extremists.html
25 https://www.dailymail.co.uk/news/article-3187428/Jeremy-Corbyn-s-links-notorious-Holocaust-denier-revealed.html
26 https://www.theguardian.com/society/2006/feb/25/localgovernment.politicsandthemedia
27 https://www.jewishvoiceforlabour.org.uk/article/our-demands-of-the-board-of-deputies-of-british-jews/
28 https://www.independent.co.uk/news/uk/politics/labour-anti-semitism-row-full-transcript-ken-livingstone-s-interviews-a7005311.html
29 https://en.wikipedia.org/wiki/Haavara_Agreement - It is also worth noting that it was Feltz who initally referred to Hitler in her questions which is why Livingstone referenced it in the first place. https://www.youtube.com/watch?v=RTFj9239fEs
30 https://www.bbc.co.uk/news/av/uk-politics-36161950

31 https://www.bbc.co.uk/news/uk-politics-36166555
32 https://www.theguardian.com/politics/2018/jul/25/jewish-newspapers-claim-corbyn-poses-existential-threat
33 See Appendix III
34 https://www.thejc.com/news/uk/corbyn-poses-an-existential-threat-to-british-jews-1.480312
35 https://www.newstatesman.com/politics/uk/2018/08/corbyn-s-zionist-remarks-were-most-offensive-enoch-powell-says-ex-chief-rabbi
36 https://www.theguardian.com/politics/video/2018/aug/24/jeremy-corbyns-2013-remarks-on-some-zionists-not-understanding-english-irony-video
37 https://en.wikipedia.org/wiki/Working_Definition_of_Antisemitism
38 https://freespeechonisrael.org.uk/ihra-opinion/
39 https://www.lrb.co.uk/the-paper/v39/n09/stephen-sedley/defining-anti-semitism
40 https://www.theguardian.com/commentisfree/2018/jul/27/antisemitism-ihra-definition-jewish-writers
41 https://www.doughtystreet.co.uk/news/ihra-definition-antisemitism-not-fit-purpose
42 https://en.wikipedia.org/wiki/New_antisemitism
43 https://www.holocaustremembrance.com/working-definition-antisemitism
44 These examples are "accusing Jewish people of being more loyal to Israel", "suggesting Israel's existence is racist", "holding Israel to a higher standard than other countries" and "comparing Israeli policies to those of the Nazis".
45 https://www.bbc.co.uk/news/uk-politics-44863606
46 https://www.thejc.com/news/uk/ihra-antisemitism-keir-starmer-jeremy-corbyn-labour-andrew-marr-1.466772
47 https://www.theguardian.com/world/2018/jul/11/labour-jewish-affiliate-in-row-with-party-over-anti-semitism-code
48 https://en.wikipedia.org/wiki/Working_Definition_of_Antisemitism#Adoption
49 https://www.researchprofessionalnews.com/rr-news-uk-universities-2020-12-more-universities-adopt-ihra-antisemitism-definition/

50 https://jewishnews.timesofisrael.com/greens-to-debate-ihra-definition-and-support-for-bds/
51 https://www.theguardian.com/news/2021/feb/12/ucl-board-rejects-ihra-definition-of-antisemitism
52 https://www.theguardian.com/commentisfree/2018/jul/18/labour-antisemitism-code-jeremy-corbyn
53 https://www.theguardian.com/politics/2018/sep/04/labour-adopts-ihra-antisemitism-definition-in-full
54 https://www.opendemocracy.net/en/opendemocracyuk/code-of-conduct-for-antisemitism-tale-of-two-texts/
55 https://talkradio.co.uk/news/chris-williamson-nec-should-add-caveat-ihra-examples-preserve-freedom-speech-18090427740
56 https://www.jewishvoiceforlabour.org.uk/article/ditch-the-ihra-definition-fight-racism-together/
57 https://www.theguardian.com/commentisfree/2019/dec/13/antisemitism-executive-order-trump-chilling-effect

Chapter 2 – The Strange Tale of Luciana Berger

58 https://www.independent.co.uk/news/uk/politics/tom-watson-luciana-berger-labour-antisemitism-chris-williamson-a8800946.html
59 https://www.liverpoolecho.co.uk/news/liverpool-news/luciana-berger-takes-liverpool-test-3435014
60 https://www.liverpoolecho.co.uk/news/liverpool-news/royle-family-star-ricky-tomlinson-3430478
61 https://www.independent.co.uk/news/uk/politics/crash-landing-for-labour-candidate-parachuted-into-liverpool-1951962.html
62 https://www.politicshome.com/news/article/clp-tells-luciana-berger-to-apologise-and-get-on-board-with-jeremy-corbyn-project
63 https://www.bbc.co.uk/news/uk-politics-47169929
64 https://inews.co.uk/news/luciana-berger-independent-group-labour-party-split-anti-semitism-announcement-video-259603
65 The four were: Garron Helm; Joshua Bonehill-Paine; John Nimmo; and Jack Coulson.
66 https://www.independent.co.uk/news/uk/politics/luciana-berger-labour-antisemitism-jeremy-corbyn-election-latest-liberal-democrats-finchley-a9196696.html

Lee Garratt | 211

Chapter 3 – Chris Williamson – The Making of a Socialist

67 https://www.shrewsbury24campaign.org.uk/history/building-trade-in-1972/
68 https://thelionandunicorn.wordpress.com/2018/04/09/a-somebody/
69 Garratt ascertained while in conversation with Williamson
70 https://core.ac.uk/download/pdf/288371365.pdf
71 https://labourlist.org/2010/02/ppc-profile-chris-williamson/

72 https://fabians.org.uk/what-happened-to-the-green-surge/
73 https://hansard.parliament.uk/commons/2011-11-01/debates/1111025000002/WorldVeganDay
74 https://morningstaronline.co.uk/article/unnatural-farm-conditions-risk-creation-new-%E2%80%98superbugs%E2%80%99
75 Emilie Oldknow was highlighted in the 851-page internal Labour Party report that was leaked in April 2020 and named as one of the senior party staff members who had allegedly tried to sabotage Labour's 2017 general election campaign. In 2018, Oldknow was appointed as assistant general secretary for the public sector union, UNISON and, before the leaked report, she was tipped as Keir Starmer's preferred replacement for Jennie Formby as Labour's general secretary. But the revelations contained in the leaked report resulted in her being suspended by the Labour Party, which ruled her out as candidate for the general secretary's role (although she was subsequently reinstated as a party member at the beginning of February 2021).

76 The Campaign for Labour Party Democracy, the CLPD, was formed in 1973
77 https://www.theguardian.com/politics/2018/jul/09/labour-mp-chris-williamson-democracy-roadshow-mandatory-reselection
78 Woodcock went on to urge people to vote Conservatives in the 2019 election. In what is surely a totally unconnected development, he received a peerage from PM Boris Johnson in 2020: https://www.independent.co.uk/news/uk/politics/general-election-john-woodcock-back-boris-johnson-tories-corbyn-labour-a9190421.html
79 https://www.theguardian.com/politics/2018/jul/09/labour-mp-chris-williamson-democracy-roadshow-mandatory-reselection
80 The bulk of the PLP had not stopped kicking themselves over what they now realised was a massive strategical error in letting Corbyn on to the initial leadership ballot. They were determined to not let this

happen again and were quite happy to side-line any internal democracy by, for example, not allowing the reducing (or getting rid of entirely as Williamson suggested) any required 'threshold' of MP support for any aspiring candidate.

81 https://www.theguardian.com/politics/2017/aug/28/make-labour-leadership-rules-more-democratic-urges-shadow-minister

82 https://www.bbc.co.uk/news/uk-40457212

83 https://www.theguardian.com/politics/2017/aug/28/make-labour-leadership-rules-more-democratic-urges-shadow-minister

84 https://www.thejc.com/news/uk/chris-williamson-posts-fake-mandela-quote-linking-israel-with-apartheid-1.443744

85 https://www.middleeasteye.net/news/nelson-mandela-30-years-palestine

86 http://www.mandela.gov.za/mandela_speeches/1997/971204_palestinian.htm

87 https://archive.vn/cKvsV#selection-569.19-569.223

88 https://archive.fo/miS1B#selection-2399.30-2411.197

89 https://antisemitism.org/politics/labour/chris-williamson/

90 https://antisemitism.org/barometer/#2018-2019

91 Just one example of many: https://www.theguardian.com/news/2021/jan/17/half-of-british-jews-will-not-display-public-sign-of-judaism

92 https://inews.co.uk/news/politics/jeremy-corbyn-anti-semite-racist-labour-177905

93 https://archive.vn/nvp1l#selection-431.147-461.205

94 Billy Bragg's comments, here, on Hodge's much feted role in Barking are interesting. https://morningstaronline.co.uk/article/stand-down-margaret

95 https://news.sky.com/story/labour-anti-semitism-row-corbyn-ally-brands-hodges-complaints-absurd-and-hyperbolic-11475129

96 https://jewishnews.timesofisrael.com/chris-williamson-shares-platform-with-expelled-anti-zionist-tony-greenstein/

97 https://archive.vn/NQXiP

98 The reader with more time on his/her hands could do worse than look at Atzmon in more detail: https://en.wikipedia.org/wiki/Gilad_Atzmon would be a good start point.

99 The roll call of Jewish people accused of antisemitism is a long and confusing one - see Appendix ??

100
https://en.wikipedia.org/wiki/Gilad_Atzmon#Allegations_of_antisemi
tism
101
https://nymag.com/intelligencer/2011/09/john_mearsheimer_ready_fo
r_ros.html
102 https://jewishnews.timesofisrael.com/jewish-students-told-dont-
study-at-lse-by-board-president/
103 https://www.politicshome.com/news/article/chris-williamson-
forced-to-apologise-for-defending-musician-accused-of-antisemitism
104 And trended at No.1 on Twitter for a while which gives a clue as
to how effective and visible these attacks against the left were
105
https://twitter.com/derbychrisw/status/1076086750697717761?lang=e
n
106 https://www.independent.co.uk/news/uk/politics/chris-
williamson-labour-mp-antisemitism-video-jeremy-corbyn-
momentum-a8798581.html
107 https://www.theguardian.com/commentisfree/2019/feb/27/labour-
chris-williamson-antisemitism
108 https://hansard.parliament.uk/Commons/2019-02-
27/debates/29279E4A-C05F-4397-BA73-
054E73A0B26D/Engagements
109 https://www.theguardian.com/politics/2019/feb/27/labour-
suspends-chris-williamson-over-antisemitism-remarks
110 https://www.theguardian.com/politics/2019/feb/27/labour-mp-
chris-williamson-party-too-apologetic-over-antisemitism-complaints
111
https://twitter.com/TribuneMPs/status/1100802591754276864/photo/
1
112 https://witchhuntfilm.org/
113 https://www.thecanary.co/uk/2018/09/25/breaking-bomb-threat-
disrupts-screening-of-film-by-israel-critic-jackie-walker-2/
114 Walker, P, 'Labour MP faces party censure after antisemitism
film', *The Guardian,* 27th February 2019:
https://www.theguardian.com/politics/2019/feb/26/labour-mp-chris-
williamson-faces-criticism-over-film-about-antisemitism-in-the-party
115 See this by the JVL as a brilliant dissection of one such article:
https://www.jewishvoiceforlabour.org.uk/article/the-curious-case-of-
jonathan-freedland/
116 See Appendix IV (Chris Williamson's first letter of suspension)

117 https://labourheartlands.com/members-pass-motion-calling-for-chris-williamsons-reinstatement/
118 One is always left flabbergasted over the length of these 'investigations'. What is it that takes so long?!
119 Elgot, J, ''Disgusting': Labour fury over return of Chris Williamson', *The Guardian,* 26th June 2019: https://www.theguardian.com/politics/2019/jun/26/chris-williamson-back-in-labour-party-after-antisemitism-remarks
120 https://www.jewishlabour.uk/
121 https://www.theguardian.com/politics/2019/jun/28/labour-mps-make-third-attempt-to-censure-chris-williamson
122 https://www.bbc.co.uk/news/uk-politics-50252630

Chapter 4 – High Court – Justice Served?

123 See Appendix VI (Chris Williamson's second letter of suspension)
124 https://news.sky.com/story/margaret-hodge-labour-investigation-made-me-think-about-treatment-of-jews-in-1930s-germany-11474295
125 https://skwawkbox.org/2018/08/18/video-finkelsteins-damning-response-to-hodge-full-version/
126 https://www.thejc.com/news/uk/suspended-mp-chris-williamson-condemned-for-plans-to-speak-at-events-at-party-conference-1.487181
127 https://www.independent.co.uk/news/uk/politics/chris-williamson-labour-conference-suspended-antisemitism-jewish-jeremy-corbyn-a9039106.html
128 https://skwawkbox.org/2018/10/27/board-of-deputies-president-accused-of-using-antisemitic-trope/
129 https://unherd.com/2019/07/is-chris-williamson-an-antisemite/
130 https://www.nytimes.com/2018/10/27/us/active-shooter-pittsburgh-synagogue-shooting.html
131 The interested reader should refer to Appendices V & VII at this point where one can see Williamson's responses, point by point, to the allegations used by the Labour Party to justify the February and September 2019 suspensions
132 https://www.bindmans.com/news/court-finds-labour-party-treated-chris-williamson-mp-unfairly-in-reopening-case-and-referring-him-to-the-ncc

133 https://www.theguardian.com/politics/2019/oct/10/chris-williamson-loses-legal-bid-over-labour-party-antisemitism-suspension
134 https://www.itv.com/news/2019-10-10/mp-chris-williamson-loses-high-court-battle-to-be-reinstated-to-labour-party
135 https://www.bbc.co.uk/news/uk-england-derbyshire-50002636
136 For the nine days from the date of the Labour Party's letter outlining their further allegations up to the day of the court hearing, the judge awarded Williamson a further 30% of the costs.
137 *1984*, George Orwell (originally published 8th June 1949)
138 Please see this link for more on the current status of the 'Left Legal Fighting Fund': https://www.fightingfund.org/donate

Chapter 5 – Starmer, Panorama and the Leaked Report

139 https://www.theatlantic.com/international/archive/2020/04/uk-labour-keir-starmer-jeremy-corbyn-anti-semitism/609685/
140 Some saw her position in the party as an attempt by Starmer to build a broad political church; RLB seen as a prominent member of the left who had, for a while, carried the hopes of the left as a potential leader.
141 https://www.independent.co.uk/arts-entertainment/films/features/maxine-peake-interview-labour-corbyn-keir-starmer-black-lives-matter-a9583206.html
142 https://twitter.com/rlong_bailey/status/1276161736148750337?lang=en
143 There is some debate on this. See the following: https://www.channel4.com/news/factcheck/factcheck-did-israeli-secret-service-teach-floyd-police-to-kneel-on-neck
144 https://www.theguardian.com/politics/2020/jun/25/keir-starmer-sacks-rebecca-long-bailey-from-shadow-cabinet
145 https://www.bbc.co.uk/iplayer/episode/m0006p8c/panorama-is-labour-antisemitic
146 https://www.bbc.co.uk/news/uk-politics-48929244
147 https://www.youtube.com/watch?v=ceCOhdgRBoc
148 https://www.theguardian.com/commentisfree/2019/apr/03/israel-treatment-palestinians-apartheid-south-africa
149 The same Louise Ellman who, in 2016, in her role as the vice chair of Labour Friends of Israel (LFI), had criticised the Oxford University Labour Club's (OULC) decision to support an 'Israel

Apartheid week', describing the comparison of Israel to South Africa as a 'grotesque smear'.

150 https://www.jewishvoiceforlabour.org.uk/article/louise-ellman-and-the-war-on-riverside-labour-party-jvl-exclusive/

151 https://www.theguardian.com/media/2019/oct/31/bbc-to-reject-labour-complaint-panorama-antisemitism-episode

152 https://labourlist.org/2019/07/full-text-labour-complaint-letter-to-bbc-about-panorama-antisemitism-episode/

153 https://morningstaronline.co.uk/article/b/starmer-facing-furious-backlash-after-caving-into-panorama-whistleblowers - the seven litigants / GLU employees were: Katherine Buckingham, Michael Creighton, Samuel Matthews, Daniel Hogan, Louise Withers Green, Martha Robinson and Benjamin Westerman

154 Quotes inside the leaked Labour dossier (first reported by Tom Rayner of Sky News on Twitter 11 April 2020) no longer available online, but see:
https://www.theguardian.com/commentisfree/2020/apr/13/labour-leaked-report-party-unity-keir-starmer-corbyn-faction &
https://en.wikipedia.org/wiki/The_work_of_the_Labour_Party%27s_Governance_and_Legal_Unit_in_relation_to_antisemitism,_2014%E2%80%932019

155 https://labourlist.org/2020/04/internal-report-lays-bare-poor-handling-of-complaints-by-labour/

156 https://www.wsws.org/en/articles/2020/04/27/labo-a27.html

157 https://www.thejc.com/news/uk/mccluskey-threatens-review-of-labour-funding-after-payout-to-antisemitism-whistleblowers-1.502187

Chapter 6 – The EHRC Report

158 https://www.theguardian.com/politics/2019/may/28/equality-body-launches-investigation-of-labour-antisemitism-claims

159 https://www.equalityhumanrights.com/en/publication-download/investigation-antisemitism-labour-party

160 https://www.opendemocracy.net/en/opendemocracyuk/american-jewish-scholar-behind-labour-s-antisemitism-scanda/

161 https://www.theguardian.com/politics/2020/oct/29/key-findings-of-the-ehrc-inquiry-into-labour-antisemitism

162 https://www.bbc.co.uk/news/av/uk-politics-54734688

163 https://www.huffingtonpost.co.uk/entry/ehrc-report-labour-reactions-anti-semitism_uk

164 https://www.facebook.com/330250343871/posts/my-statement-following-the-publication-of-the-ehrc-reportantisemitism-is-absolut/10158939532253872/
165 https://labourlist.org/2020/11/rayner-says-thousands-of-labour-members-may-be-suspended-from-party/
166 "It is not legitimate for the leadership to influence, make recommendations or make decisions on complaints."
167 https://www.jewishvoiceforlabour.org.uk/article/saying-the-quiet-part-out-loud/
168 https://jewishnews.timesofisrael.com/labour-suspends-local-chair-after-unacceptable-atmosphere-at-online-meeting/
169 https://www.jewishvoiceforlabour.org.uk/article/nottingham-east-members-defend-suspended-clp-chair/
170 https://mobile.twitter.com/AmmarKazmi_/status/1332686403113791489
171 https://skwawkbox.org/2020/11/25/outraged-jewish-members-accuse-labour-of-weaponising-them-to-kill-free-speech-as-party-uses-safe-space-to-threaten-clps-over-corbyn-motions/

Chapter 7 – With Friends Like These

172 https://electronicintifada.net/blogs/david-cronin/how-guardian-told-me-steer-clear-palestine
173 https://www.theguardian.com/commentisfree/2018/apr/01/if-corbyn-is-not-to-appear-a-passenger-he-must-learn-to-lead
174 https://www.theguardian.com/commentisfree/2019/mar/04/labour-antisemitism-party-left-bigotry
175 https://www.theguardian.com/commentisfree/2019/apr/02/gary-lineker-luciana-berger-trolls-trolled-social-media-abuse
176 The articles listed here are the tip of the iceberg when it comes to biased and misleading Guardian reporting. See: https://theguardian.fivefilters.org/antisemitism/
177 https://www.theguardian.com/politics/2019/feb/20/jeremy-corbyn-labour-party-crucial-ally-in-fight-against-antisemitism
178 https://mronline.org/2019/07/12/the-guardian-publishes-then-censors-jewish-open-letter-defending-smeared-pro-corbyn-labour-mp-chris-williamson/
179 https://twitter.com/kennardmatt/status/1147064458537263104

180 https://www.theguardian.com/info/2019/jul/09/removed-article
181 https://www.pressgazette.co.uk/steve-bell-leaves-the-guardian/
182 https://www.theguardian.com/commentisfree/2017/apr/21/steve-bell-and-antisemitism
183 https://www.theguardian.com/commentisfree/2020/nov/12/cartoon-reader-complaints-steve-bell-former-labour-leader-head-plate
184 Owen Jones, *This Land*, Penguin, p.78-80, 224, 251-256

Conclusion with Finkelstein

185 https://www.youtube.com/watch?v=JEX5OGmXLz4
186 https://www.theguardian.com/uk-news/2019/feb/23/liverpool-wavertree-labour-constituency-antisemitism-luciana-berger-derek-hatton
187 https://www.thesun.co.uk/news/8413769/what-are-the-figures-about-reported-antisemitism-released-by-the-labour-party/
188 https://publications.parliament.uk/pa/cm201617/cmselect/cmhaff/136/136.pdf
189 https://www.jpr.org.uk/publication?id=9993
190 https://www.scmp.com/article/970657/not-letting-facts-ruin-good-story
191 https://twitter.com/jeremycorbyn/status/1333062122117492739?lang=en
192 https://skwawkbox.org/2020/11/30/redbridge-labour-deletes-tweet-calling-corbyns-solidarity-with-palestinians-anti-jewish/

Afterword

193 https://youtu.be/wB8EMRgVV1U
194 https://electronicintifada.net/blogs/asa-winstanley/we-slaughtered-jeremy-corbyn-says-israel-lobbyist
195 https://www.bod.org.uk/when-he-eventually-steps-back-history-will-not-look-kindly-on-jeremy-corbyns-leadership-of-the-labour-party-where-anti-jewish-racism-has-been-allowed-to-run-amok/
196 https://www.facebook.com/TheDailyPolitik/videos/576578343123325

197 http://www.britishpoliticalspeech.org/speech-archive.htm?speech=212

198 https://www.survation.com/clients/we-own-it/

199 https://www.youtube.com/watch?v=W7lsRbDKOXg

200 https://www.theguardian.com/politics/2016/sep/27/jeremy-corbyns-team-targets-labour-membership-one-million

201 https://electronicintifada.net/blogs/asa-winstanley/jewish-labour-movement-was-refounded-fight-corbyn

202 https://www.politicshome.com/news/article/jewish-labour-movement-says-it-will-not-campaign-to-make-jeremy-corbyn-prime-minister

203 https://www.aljazeera.com/news/2017/1/13/uk-corbyn-calls-for-probe-into-israeli-interference

204 https://electronicintifada.net/blogs/asa-winstanley/keir-starmer-tilts-labour-sharply-towards-israel

205 https://isreview.org/issue/108/morbid-symptoms

206 https://www.acorntheunion.org.uk/

207 https://palestineaction.org/faqs/

208 https://www.resistmovement.org.uk/

Appendix I & II

209 https://www.jewishvoiceforlabour.org.uk/article/formal-complaint-to-labour-over-speeches-leaked-to-jewish-chronicle/

210 https://www.thejc.com/news/uk/labour-suspends-senior-jvl-official-after-deeply-unpleasant-meeting-1.509331

211 https://www.thejc.com/news/uk/israeli-born-anti-zionist-expelled-from-labour-party-1.445722

212 https://www.jewishvoiceforlabour.org.uk/article/branch-motions-resolutions-expulsion-moshe-machover/

213 https://weeklyworker.co.uk/worker/1173/expelled-for-saying-the-unsayable/

214 https://electronicintifada.net/blogs/asa-winstanley/labour-purges-veteran-israeli-anti-zionist-moshe-machover

Appendix V

215 https://www.theguardian.com/politics/2018/sep/25/jewish-event-at-labour-conference-abandoned-after-bomb-scare

216 https://youtu.be/L3dn-VV3czc?t=19
217 https://electronicintifada.net/content/jeremy-corbyn-must-stop-pandering-labours-israel-lobby/23731
218 https://www.youtube.com/watch?v=L7SOa6drbBI

219 https://www.ft.com/content/6ea6ef26-5454-11e9-91f9-b6515a54c5b1
220 https://skwawkbox.org/2018/09/06/breaking-ryan-loses-no-confidence-vote/
221 https://twitter.com/joanryanEnfield/status/1037827090723340289
222 https://skwawkbox.org/2018/06/11/excl-enfield-caliskan-scandal-grows-all-black-councillors-were-deselected/
223 https://skwawkbox.org/2019/03/08/breaking-enfield-council-labour-group-dramatically-banned-from-meeting-by-nec/
224 https://youtu.be/L3dn-VV3czc?t=461
225 https://electronicintifada.net/blogs/asa-winstanley/how-israel-lobby-fakes-anti-semitism
226 https://youtu.be/Vuk1EhkEctE?t=412
227 https://www.jpost.com/Diaspora/UKs-Corbyn-calls-for-investigation-into-Israels-meddling-after-embassy-row-478585
228 https://www.middleeasteye.net/news/israel-embassy-plot-labour-pushes-inquiry-shai-masot-scandal
229 https://electronicintifada.net/blogs/asa-winstanley/israel-lobby-funders-back-breakaway-british-mps
230 https://jewishnews.timesofisrael.com/joan-ryan-tells-aipac-labour-seeks-to-demonise-and-delegitimise-israel/
231
https://twitter.com/edwardpoole1975/status/1117411772141535232
232
https://twitter.com/AdamMcGibbon/status/1117695251097899008
233 https://twitter.com/AlastairJT/status/1076089250335080448
234 https://electronicintifada.net/content/fake-labour-accounts-fueling-anti-semitism-crisis/26441
235 https://twitter.com/magnitsky Iggy Ostanin has deleted the reference in his biography to his employer, Bellingcat, after it was revealed (https://www.rt.com/uk/454844-integrity-initiative-leaks-expose-network/) recently that the company was involved in a £10m funding bid to the FCO to take part in an information warfare campaign. He is the 'source' for several media stories targeting Jeremy Corbyn as a 'threat to national security' and intimating that Jeremy himself is an anti-Semite.

236 https://metro.co.uk/2018/07/18/labour-mp-turns-jeremy-corbyn-calling-fing-anti-semite-racist-7729431/

237 https://www.mirror.co.uk/news/politics/jeremy-corbyn-blasts-margaret-hodge-14094497

238 https://www.thetimes.co.uk/article/corbyn-hit-by-mutiny-on-airstrikes-wgrvzpt30ld

239 https://www.thetimes.co.uk/article/former-head-of-mi6-sir-richard-dearlove-troubled-by-corbyn-m85vxbkbz

240 https://www.msn.com/en-ae/news/other/corbyn-e2-80-99s-closest-adviser-is-national-security-risk-says-former-mi6-chief/ar-BBTZll2

241 https://www.thetimes.co.uk/article/mi5-head-andrew-parker-summons-jeremy-corbyn-for-facts-of-life-talk-on-terror-vwxncthlf

242 https://www.thetimes.co.uk/article/brexit-weary-britons-long-for-political-strongman-wwl86hcqq

243 http://www.lse.ac.uk/media@lse/research/pdf/JeremyCorbyn/Cobyn-Report-FINAL.pdf

244 https://www.mediareform.org.uk/wp-content/uploads/2016/07/Corbynresearch.pdf

245 https://d25d2506sfb94s.cloudfront.net/cumulus_uploads/document/pvxdr2lh73/InternalResults_160830_LabourSelectorate.pdf

246 https://www.jewishsocialist.org.uk/news/item/statement-on-labours-problem-with-antisemitism-from-the-jewish-socialists-g

247 https://www.theguardian.com/politics/2018/apr/02/stop-jeremy-corbyns-trial-by-media-over-antisemitism

248 https://labourlist.org/2016/10/chuka-umunna-clause-iv-tells-us-to-live-in-solidarity-tolerance-and-respect-but-labour-has-failed-to-deliver/

249 https://www.independent.co.uk/voices/labour-party-antisemitism-jeremy-corbyn-chuka-umunna-windrush-a8318436.html

250 https://labourlist.org/2019/03/siobhain-mcdonagh-links-anti-capitalism-to-antisemitism-in-labour/

251 https://www.youtube.com/watch?v=5fpaBaoN_jw&app=desktop

252 https://jewishnews.timesofisrael.com/chris-williamson-accused-of-whitewashing-prejudices-by-signing-holocaust-book/

253 https://labour.org.uk/wp-content/uploads/2017/10/Chakrabarti-Inquiry-Report-30June16.pdf

254 https://www.theguardian.com/politics/2015/aug/20/jeremy-corbyn-and-antisemitism-claims

255 https://www.thejc.com/news/uk-news/luciana-berger-targeted-by-antisemites-after-jailing-of-abusive-internet-troll-1.59652
256 https://www.independent.co.uk/news/uk/crime/luciana-berger-antisemitic-abuse-neo-nazi-man-jailed-two-year-sentence-a7463726.html
257 https://www.liverpoolecho.co.uk/news/liverpool-news/jail-internet-troll-who-told-12588883
258 https://www.thejc.com/news/uk-news/luciana-berger-murder-boast-terror-offences-trial-1.467449

Appendix VIII

259 https://en.wikipedia.org/wiki/Niran
260 https://www.haaretz.com/who-s-throwing-who-into-the-sea-1.5202302
261
https://en.wikipedia.org/wiki/Truth_and_Reconciliation_Commission_(South_Africa)

Index

Abbott, Diane, 112, 186

Anidjar, Gil, 6

Atzmon, Gilad, 54-57, 113, 153-155, 172

Austin, Ian, 97, 111, 159-160

Balls, Ed, 128

Barazetti, Bill, 136

Beckett, Margaret, 45

Beeley, Vanessa, 157

Begin, Menachem, 146

Bell, Steve, 109-110

Ben-Gurion, David, 8

Benn, Hilary, 111

Benn, Tony, 112, 125-126

Berger, Luciana, 33-38, 46, 58, 94, 105-106, 119, 170-171

Bindman, Geoffrey, 25

Blair, Euan, 33

Blair, Tony, 33, 48, 127

Bonehill-Paine, Joshua, 170

Bookbinder, David, 40

Bragg, Billy, 212

Brandreth, Gyles, 128

Bromley, Pam, 92-94

Buckingham, Katherine, 216

Burgon, Richard, 79

Caplin, Ivor, 56

Carroll, Lewis, 91

Chakrabarti, Shami, 108, 166-167

Chilcot, John, 111, 159

Chomsky, Noam, 108, 118

Clark, Katy, 88

Clay, Cassius, 76

Cleverly, James, 59

Corbyn, Jeremy, throughout

Cotler, Irwin, 26

Coulson, Jack, 171

Creighton, Michael, 85

Cronin, David, 104

Dearlove, Richard, 161

Dugher, Michael, 15

Eisen, Paul, 18

Ellman, Louise, 86

Evans, David, 99

Falter, Gideon, 91

Feltz, Vanessa, 21

Finegold, Oliver, 19

Finkelstein, Norman, 72, 92, 117-118, 181-182

Fisk, Robert, 197

Fitzpatrick, Jean, 167

Floyd, George, 82-83

Ford, Peter, 157

Forde, Martin, 204-205

Formby, Jennie, 59, 62-64, 67-69, 72, 75, 95, 143, 162

Freedland, Jonathan, 58, 63, 85, 104-105

Galilei, Galileo, 117-118

Galloway, George, 205

Gerber, Jennifer, 56

Gilligan, Andrew, 17-18

Glasman, Joe, 125

Gramsci, Antonio, 130

Green, Louise Withers, 216

Greenstein, Tony, 186-187, 190

Gregson, Peter, 190

Hadfield, Greg, 186

Hamilton, Fabian, 67

Harman, Harriet, 128

Harris, John, 105

Hartley-Brewer, Julia, 170

Healey, Denis, 127

Helm, Garron, 170-171

Hitler, Adolf, 21, 84, 105, 170-171

Hodge, Margaret, 11, 39, 53, 72, 94, 111, 159-160, 164-165, 174, 181-182

Hoffman, Jonathan, 146

Hogan, Daniel, 89

Hubble, John, 35

Icke, David, 178

Irving, David, 136

Jackson, Amy, 58

Jansson, Asa, 186

Johnson, Alan, 85

Johnson, Boris, 69, 73, 109

Jones, Owen, 13, 110-115

Judaken, Jonathan, 5-7

Kafka, Franz, 69, 81, 101, 117

Kazmi, Ammar, 217

Khan, Sadiq, 94

Kinnock, Neil, 127

Kinnock, Stephen, 29-30

Klug, Brian, 29

Lavery, Ian, 159

Leadbeater, Kim, 205

Leigh, Mike, 61

Lenszner, Damon, 146

Leslie, Chris, 36-37

Lewis, Clive, 167

Lewis, Helen, 104-105

Liston, Sonny, 76

Livingstone, Ken, 3, 19-22, 92-94, 109, 119

Loach, Ken, 87

Long-Bailey, Rebecca, 82-84

Machiavelli, Niccolò, 57, 113

Machover, Moshé, 134-135, 167

Maguire, Kevin, 151

Mandela, Nelson, 49-50, 166

Mandelson, Peter, 98

Mann, John, 22, 134

Mao, Chairman, 110

Marr, Andrew, 28

Marr, Wilhelm, 5

Masot, Shai, 85, 129, 152

Matthews, Sam, 88, 134

May, Theresa, 16, 59, 129

McCarthy, Joseph, 98, 121

McCluskey, Len, 90

McDonagh, Siobhain, 164-165

McDonnell, John, 36, 89, 97, 112

McGahey, Mick, 122

McGuinness, Martin, 16

Meacher, Michael, 43

Melvin, Melanie, 186-187

Miliband, Ed, 15, 43, 60, 112, 127-128

Miliband, Ralph, 138

Mills, Tom, 160

Milne, Seumas, 58, 78, 85

Mirvis, Ephraim, 95

Morris, Grahame, 44

Mortimer, Jill, 205

Mosley, Oswald, 150

Murphy, Karie, 58-59, 64, 88

Nelson, Scott, 180

Netanyahu, Benjamin, 17, 109, 121

Nietzsche, Friedrich, 13, 103

Nimmo, John, 171

Oberman, Tracy-Ann, 105

Oldknow, Emilie, 44

One, Mear, 92

Orwell, George, 54, 77, 101, 150

Othello, 33

Paisley, Ian, 138

Parker, Andrew, 161

Peake, Maxine, 82-83

Peled, Miko, 113

Pepperall, Edward, 74-75, 78

Phillips, Jess, 67

Pidcock, Laura, 67, 179

Powell, Enoch, 24

Putin, Vladimir, 46

Rachman, Gideon, 147

Rayner, Angela, 97, 119

Rayner, Tom, 216

Regan, Louise, 99, 101

Regev, Mark, 129

Robertson, Geoffrey, 25

Robinson, Martha, 216

Rose, Ella, 85, 145

Ryan, Joan, 23, 30, 150-151

Sacks, Jonathan, 23-24

Samsa, Gregor, 117

Secker, Glyn, 167

Sedley, Stephen, 25

Segalov, Michael, 11, 57

Shah, Naz , 92-93

Shankly, Bill , 34, 46

Smeeth, Ruth , 62, 67, 72-73

Smith, John , 127

Smith, Laura , 67

Smith, Winston, , 77

Starmer, Keir , 28, 81-84, 87, 94, 96, 129

Stephenson, Ryan, 205

Stern, Kenneth, 31

Streeting, Wes, 28, 72-73

Tant, Millie, 39

Tatchell, Peter, 157

Thatcher, Margaret, 48

Thompson, Alastair, 153

Thornberry, Emily, 152, 159, 163

Tomlinson, Hugh, 25

Tomlinson, Ricky, 34-35

Trump, Donald, 109

Tutu, Desmond, 86

Umunna, Chuka, 36-37, 164

Underwood, Ken, 179

Van der Zyl, Marie, 125, 156

Vaz, Keith, 67-68, 74, 167

Wadsworth, Marc, 53, 166-167

Walker, Jackie, 61-62, 85, 145, 179-180, 185

Ware, John, 84, 87

Watson, Tom, 11, 22, 33, 36, 60, 85, 107, 109

Wayne, Naomi, 169

Westerman, Benjamin, 216

Whittome, Nadia, 98-99, 101

Wiesenthal, Simon, 136

Williams, Paul, 205

Williamson, Chris, throughout

Williamson, Gavin, 29

Wimborne-Idrissi, Naomi, 133

Winstanley, Asa, 57

Woodcock, John, 46

Woodward, Shaun, 34

Printed in Great Britain
by Amazon